A Prospect of
Sutherland

A Prospect of
Sutherland

*The Building of a Castle and the
Making of a Duchess*

Gilbert T. Bell

Birlinn

This edition published by
Birlinn Ltd
13 Roseneath Street
Edinburgh EH9 1JH

Copyright © Gilbert T. Bell 1995

ISBN 1 874744 25 4

A CIP record for this book is available from the
British Library

Designed and Typeset by Image & Print Group, Glasgow
Typeset in 10 pt Palatino

Made and printed in Finland by WSOY

Contents

Part Four – A View to Sutherland

List of Ilustrations

Acknowledgements

In writing anything debts of gratitude are due – in writing anything historical or topographical debts of gratitude are many. In writing on something with as many and as diverse strands to it as this tale the debts of thanks are very many indeed. To all who deserve my thanks I now offer it most gratefully and sincerely. No one therefore ought to feel that they have been overlooked even if space does not permit them all to be named.

I am most grateful to all the many authors whose books and articles were consulted and whose information proved valuable on so many of the issues and problems encountered in these pages. Writers would not get very far if they did not rely heavily on those who went before – this work has benefited greatly by being able to draw on a rich resource of literature. My debt in particular to Sir Walter Scott will be quite obvious throughout. Chapter 10 benefited enormously from Sir Arthur Conan Doyle's writings, whose model Victorian detective would no doubt have relished the investigation and doubtless have produced a more satisfactory solution to the problem.

Some people merit a very special word of thanks. These include Mrs Elizabeth Beaton, formerly an Inspector of Historic Buildings, John Gifford of the *Buildings of Scotland* Research Unit, Ian Gow of the National Monuments Record of Scotland, David Walker, formerly of Historic Scotland, and the Director and Staff of the Planning Department of Highland Regional Council. Many Planning Departments south of the Border were most helpful especially Michael Ray, Director of Planning, of the Borough of Hove, and Elizabeth Long of the Forward Planning Unit, Royal Borough of Windsor and Maidenhead.

Libraries, librarians and archivists, too numerous to mention and from far and wide, have been of immense assistance. Many individuals, however, merit special mention. These include Ms Deborah Eaton, Librarian at St Edmund

Hall, Oxford; Miss C. A. Goodfellow and Mrs M. Williams of Inverness Library; Miss J. Crowther of Hull's Central Library; David Bromwich, Local History Librarian at Taunton; T.B. Groom of Staffordshire Record Office; Karen Standage of Hove Central Library; Duncan Mirylees at Guildford Library; Stuart McLean of Sutherland Registrars Office, Brora; Robert Steward, Regional Archivist of Highland Regional Council; Adam Spencer, archivist, at the Grange Museum, Neasden; Martin Tupper of Islington Central Library, Kathryn McCord of Kensington's Central Library and Jim Henderson and his staff at the *Northern Times*, Golspie.

The Chambers of Commerce of Tarpon Springs and Dunedin were most helpful as was Barbara Skubish of Dunedin Public Library but very special thanks are due to Marilyn Ady of Tarpon Springs Library. The State of Florida Department of Commerce, Division of Tourism was also a source of useful information. I also have to thank the Cyprus Tourist Office, the Press and Information Office of the Cyprus High Commission, the Egyptian Press and Information Bureau, the Egyptian Tourist Authority, and the Tourism Authority of Thailand, as well as the High Commission of India and in particular Miss M. S. Travis, the Librarian at India House.

The vicars, rectors, ministers and churchwardens in many churches were very generous in their help but the Rev. Stephen Hotchen of St Anne's Strathpeffer and Rev. James Simpson of Dornoch Cathedral, now Moderator of the General Assembly of the Church of Scotland, deserve my special thanks.

I must express particular thanks to the Countess of Sutherland, Ian Cadell of Mining and Chemical Products (the former owners of Foliejon Park), Nigel Clutton of Messrs Cluttons, Nigel Connor and Trentham Gardens, Derek Conran of Hertford College, Oxford, Robert Copeland, formerly of Tittensor Chase, and Mr Bellack presently of Tittensor Chase, Kirk Wolley Dod of Messrs Taylor Joynson and Garrett (successors to Taylor and Humbert), Sir Gerald

Elliot (of the Salvesen family) and Messrs Christian Salvesen plc, Ian Forshaw of the Forestry Commission (Scotland), the Frost Partnership of Windsor, John Hacker of the Willows Riverside Park, Windsor, Michael Ketchin of Dornoch Castle Hotel, Shaun Longsdon of Messrs Knight Frank & Rutley, A. J. Macdonald-Buchanan of Inveran, Dr Ellen Macnamara of Ardgay, Vicky Maiden of Messrs Maples, Keith Massey and J. L. E. Oliver of HM Prison – Holloway, Dr M. J. Orbell of Messrs Baring Bros and Co. Ltd., John Pulford of Walton & Weybridge Local History Society, Major W. Shaw of the Royal Highland Fusiliers, Nikolai Skeie of the Norwegian Consulate General in Edinburgh, Derek Tremayne at Lilleshall and the Sports Council, Dr Deborah Turnbull, formerly Deputy Warden of Hull University's Thwaite Hall, and last but by no means least, to James Bell of Dornoch Heritage.

Above all, however, thanks are due to the Scottish Youth Hostels Association and to the Director, James Martin, for his help and encouragement. It was the SYHA magazine which first alerted my attention to Carbisdale Castle and to what I thought was a good story worthy of further research and the SYHA have been most helpful during its progress. Thanks are also due to Mr James Burgess at Carbisdale.

All these kind people have helped but at the end of the day the interpretation of facts and events is mine and all may not agree with the emphasis placed here. I hope they will forgive me for having wandered off the route originally planned as the finding of new information constantly led to new avenues to explore and more dead-ends to batter one's way through. If it is a better story thanks are due to all of them for their help whether or not they would wish to claim any involvement or not. Sadly its failings are no one's fault but my own.

It would be greatly remiss not to conclude without stating the huge debt of thanks due to my wife, Maureen, who has shared much of the burden as well as much of the pleasure in seeing this piece take shape and come to fruition in these pages. I hope she agrees that it was worth all the effort.

Foreword

Carbisdale Castle is a problem.

Most books on Scottish castles overlook it and one (Ross 1987) in under half a dozen lines, dismissed Carbisdale as a 'folly'. Perhaps not surprisingly in the few books on follies (Casson, Jones, Headey and Meulenkamp, and Mott) Carbisdale does not figure. Carbisdale Castle has, therefore, got an identity problem. The reason is simple enough – it is not a folly although it undoubtedly has elements of the folly about it. It was also built long after there was a need to build fortified houses and therefore one might reasonably conclude that it is a country house rather than a castle.

It is not as simple as that, however, for most books dealing with country houses have also tended to ignore poor Carbisdale. Presumably authors such as Forman, Girouard, Aslett, and Robinson thought it more of a castle! One of the latest books on Scottish architecture, Gifford's *Highlands and Islands*, an otherwise splendid volume, does not include Carbisdale Castle among the delights.

Carbisdale was certainly the last castle – so called – to be built in Scotland. With the exception of Devon's Castle Drogo, which was begun at roughly the same time but took substantially longer to build, it was possibly the last castle built in Britain. Certainly for size Carbisdale has its southern rival soundly beaten. At Castle Drogo, for all its grandeur, only one third of its owner's original scheme was actually built. Carbisdale, on the other hand, became a mighty citadel, completed to its owner's grand plan even if the owner did not live to see it in all its glory.

Castle Drogo was designed by Sir Edwin Lutyens, the foremost architect of his day, and is now a well-known and much loved National Trust property. It has attracted much attention and received much acclaim.

Carbisdale has been largely ignored.

One wonders why Carbisdale should have been given such scant attention. In most books, if it rates a mention at all, it receives a bare two lines compared to the ample coverage allotted to other castles and country houses, many of which are lesser buildings and have a considerably less interesting tale attached.

Carbisdale may not be a true castle in an architectural or fortified constructional sense of the term for its battlements and turrets serve no defensive role but as regards its commanding situation, its castellated stone walls, its historic site – Montrose fought his last battle there – and its romantic history it has scarce an equal among the so-called 'real' castles. It even has, reputedly, a ghost or two.

About twenty-five miles or so and about 500 years and more separate the castles of Dunrobin and Carbisdale yet the history of both will be eternally entwined. Both have been in their day a seat of the Duchess of Sutherland. Without Dunrobin there would have been no Carbisdale and in a sense without Carbisdale there would have been a very different future for Dunrobin. That Dunrobin survives in its present form is in part due to the creation of Carbisdale.

Lest the reader think the writer is indulging in a flight of fancy at best or in some high-blown hyperbole at worst let us attempt to investigate the history of the building and its owners. The reader can thus ascertain if there be substance to these claims or if indeed it is mere bombastic verbiage. Carbisdale Castle is not a 'Castle in the Air' but is rooted in reality and is worthy of serious consideration. It has a colourful and eventful past. It has an interesting and useful present. It ought to have a secure and rewarding future and its past deserves to be better known.

Introduction

*But no one shall find me rowing against the
stream. I care not who knows it – I write for the
general amusement.*

SIR WALTER SCOTT – *from The Fortunes of Nigel*

The novelist Ian Fleming might have chosen *From Ross-shire
with Love* as a title but although our story is about a castle
built in Ross-shire it is really a tale about Sutherland. It is a
strange story.

Some years ago, while on holiday in the North of Scotland, I
first became aware of the majestic mass of Carbisdale Castle,
overlooking the Kyle of Sutherland and contributing so much
to the vista. Its impressive bulk and its commanding location
made it a conspicuous feature of the landscape. Few castles
have a setting quite so grand and yet few spots needed a
castle quite so much to transform what was quite fine into
something which is quite splendid.

Vaguely aware that it had been built by a former Duchess of
Sutherland, I knew that it later had been gifted to the Scottish
Youth Hostels Association. Though a Life Member of the
SYHA I had regrettably, in my youth, never stayed in this,
their grandest of hostels and now the comforts of hotel
lounges are more appealing, if no less welcoming, than the
friendly camaraderie of hostel common rooms. As a historian
I had rather rashly dismissed Carbisdale as a modern
mansion – of no great antiquity and therefore of no great
interest.

An article in the SYHA's *Newsletter* of Winter 1991 revealed
that Carbisdale Castle did indeed have a history: it seemed
such a splendidly tantalising story one felt compelled to know
more. In delving a little deeper many conflicting accounts and
unresolved questions were discovered and all forced me to try
to get to the bottom of the story. To put the castle into context

it was thus necessary, in the words of the song, to "start at the very beginning".

What began as a little exercise in architectural history quite simply grew. As the story of Carbisdale developed, it was to become a tale of intrigue and romance, of treachery and devotion, of elegant buildings and magnificent acres, of grand ideas and lofty ambitions, but also of low morals and base actions. From its beginnings in Sutherland the story was to have a geographical spread both far and wide and from battles bloody was to culminate in battles legal. That wars are not over until the last battle has been fought and won is as true of the Carbisdale story as of any other. This was to be a yarn with very many strands to be unravelled and many mysteries to be solved. Although some of the elements of the finest of fiction were present this was historical fact.

In *The Adventures of Huckleberry Finn*, Mark Twain has written, "There was things that he stretched but mainly he told the truth. That is nothing. I never seen anybody but lied one time or another . . . " In describing his Tom Sawyer book Twain confessed it was "mostly a true book with some stretchers". I have tried to make this as true a book as possible. If there be "stretchers" may they be few – they are certainly unintentional. Most of what follows is true.

History is a bit like an old jigsaw. Like old jigsaws there are invariably one or two (or more) bits missing. Gaps exist in this story as they do in all history for, in a sense, it is impossible to tell the "whole story" of anything; all history is partial. Some of the gaps in this story may exist because of discreet pressure, both real and imagined in the past, to suppress the truth. It may be that even today the Sutherland family do not wish all the facts to be known about a painful episode in their history. In spite of the gaps, however, it is still possible to gain an impression of the overall picture and in time other pieces may be found which will help us complete the puzzle.

Hopefully, readers will agree that in spite of its fairly solid historical foundation this is a pretty good story, worth relating and worth reading.

The heroine of the story – Duchess Blair – has had a bad press – her character brutally assassinated. It is not the intention here to be sympathetic or to rescue a tarnished reputation but merely to re-assess it and, if necessary, re-rubbish it. Similarly, the other main characters who, in the past, have not suffered so cruelly at the pens of others may also find that they are neither the knights in shining armour nor the lily-white damsels we have been led to believe. The aim is to be as fair as is possible to everyone and set the record straight.

To those who would travel along the byways of history some patience is demanded, for the routes are often obscure and the views often clouded. The path is seldom straight. Signposts are misleading and obstacles both man-made and natural impede the progress and the direction and the destination are seldom clearcut. It has thus always been so in writing and perhaps more so in this saga for we are dealing with a castle in the Highlands of Scotland, not a 'castle in the air'; a piece of history, not a romantic legend.

Reader enjoy your journey, enjoy the jigsaw.

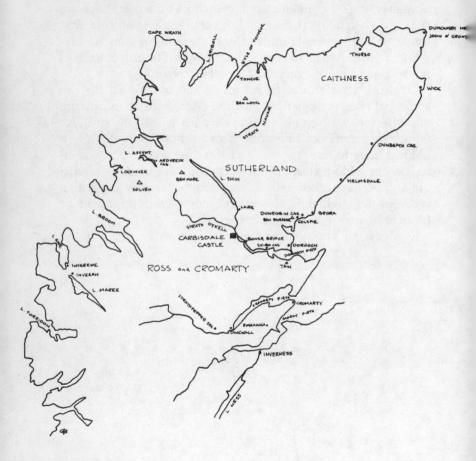

The North of Scotland

PART ONE

Mansions, Mountains and Marriages

I cannot tell how the truth may be;
I say the tale as 'twas said to me.
SIR WALTER SCOTT – from *The Lay of the Last Minstrel*

CHAPTER ONE

The House of Sutherland

Land of brown heath and shaggy wood,
Land of the mountain and the flood.
Land of my sires!
SIR WALTER SCOTT – FROM *The Lay of the Last Minstrel*

Our story begins with the word – Sutherland. It is a surname of territorial or regional origin taking its name from the vast tract of land and former county which we know as Sutherland. Immediately, however, we hit a snag, for here in the far north of Scotland is a word which is a corruption of the Norse word 'Sudrland' meaning southernland. The seafaring Norsemen had laid claim to the islands which make up Orkney and Shetland and the mainland territory of Caithness and possibly Sutherland. It was so named either because it lay to the south of land which the Norsemen had conquered in one of their colonising waves or, as seems most likely, it was itself the southern part of the Norsemen's extensive Scottish possessions of the ancient earldom of Caithness. It is interesting to note that some present day Orcadians refer to mainland Scotland as 'the Sooth' because it lies to their south.

Around the present town of Dornoch are a cluster of place names which seem to suggest Scandinavian origin – Skelbo, Skibo and Embo. It seems unlikely that the area was simply a Norse outpost beyond the southern extremity of their conquered territory but that Norse colonisation had in fact stretched as far south as the edge of what we know to be present-day Sutherland.

Sutherland has long daylight hours and a rich diversity of scene – rugged mountains, quiet lochans and rushing rivers as well as a magnificent coastline offering sea lochs, sandy bays, towering cliffs and the great Smoo Cave. The area is often referred to as being part of 'Europe's last wilderness' and it offers an unspoilt landscape of almost interminable dimensions. One writer described it thus – 'Wildness and sterility are the great features of the landscape, the dreary monotony being seldom relieved by tree or shrub; and this uniformity of desolation is only occasionally broken by some glen or strath presenting itself as an oasis of verdure in the bleak desert' (Groom, 1885, VI, 416). While this bleak generalisation has much truth in it, Sutherland has much more and a visit will prove that it has lots to interest and some change of scene. Even the uniform barrenness has a strange fascination. It is a peaceful place. In a world full of noise and bustle the quiet miles can be a welcome change.

The area may offer hundreds of square miles of desolation and isolation with a resident population few in numbers but its very inhospitability makes it a naturalists' paradise: it offers rich varieties in bird and plant life. A layer of peat covers most of the land and a few hills, some larger lochs and the broad straths relieve the overall vast emptiness. It is a place of surprises. But the straths were not always peaceful. Men fought to gain them and had to fight to keep them.

This is the eventful story of *the* Sutherland family. If a later monument, at Holyrood Abbey, is to be believed then the Sutherland family is descended from Allan, Thane of Sutherland, who was killed by Macbeth when he was attempting to secure the throne for the future Malcolm III sometime around 1057.

The present family do not trace the family quite so far back in the distant past but nonetheless the sword had its role. Possibly in 1196 the King of Scots, William the Lion, at the head of a strong army marched across the River Oykell and brought Caithness and Sutherland within the realm of the Scottish Crown. After it had been detached from the

Norsemen much of the territory, if not all of it, was given by a grateful King to Hugh Freskin of Moray, Lord Duffus, as a reward for his services. The present village and bay of Freskin, a few miles south of John o'Groats, would suggest that much of Caithness as well as Sutherland had been part of Freskin's domain. The Sutherland badge of a wild cat and the very name Caithness (or Cat-ness) might also suggest an identity link as well as a physical link between the two adjacent territories.

Freskin's family were of Flemish or Norman origin but had settled in Moray where they had received land from King David I and thus assumed the style 'de Moravia' (of Moray). Hugh seems to have become 'Lord of Sutherland' some time before 1211 and it was his son, William, who adopted the style 'of Sutherland' which in time led to the surname being adopted from that territorial name. King Alexander II made him Earl of Sutherland some time around 1230. Those who held Earldoms were in positions of great status as well as having much power and influence. Earls were by blood or prestige regarded as kinsmen of the monarch and for many centuries the fortunes of the Earls of Sutherland were linked to the fortunes of the Scottish throne.

William, 2nd Earl, fought for Robert the Bruce at Bannockburn when Scotland managed to free herself from her large southern neighbour and end what had been regarded as eighteen years of English rule by occupation and oppression. The 4th Earl was one of half a dozen earls killed alongside the Regent of Scotland at the Battle of Halidon Hill, fought near Berwick in 1333, when the Scottish army was destroyed at the hands of English bowmen. The 5th Earl fought alongside his brother-in-law, King David II, at the disastrous Battle of Neville's Cross, fought near Durham in 1346, when the Scots were routed by the English.

The 5th Earl's first wife had been Princess Margaret, elder daughter of King Robert Bruce, and his son would have succeeded to the throne had he not died during a plague in 1361. The son of Princess Marjorie Bruce, wife of Walter the

Steward, therefore took the throne on the death of David II in 1371 and thus began almost 350 years of Stuart rule. Scotland had come very close to having Sutherland rule – it would have been a very different course for Scottish history; not any better, one suspects, but just different.

Within Sutherland this family was ever the leader of society. On the old hump-backed bridge at Golspie a stone obelisk has been placed on one of its parapet walls – it is the Clan Sutherland gathering stone. With a bold-relief crown to its face and Gaelic inscription, it commemorated (or provided a rallying point for) the faithful armed service of the men from Sutherland who would rise up and fight when called upon by their Clan Chief. A loose translation of its text has it that 'The Big Man (Lord or Earl) at the head of the little bridge proclaimed his clans to the victories'. 'Ceann na Droichaide bige' (The Head of the Little Bridge) was the war cry of the clan. It is not clear when the monument was erected or indeed quite what it commemorated. Some have suggested that the battle which they fought was against the Norsemen but it seems more likely to have been inter-clan strife and the monument was erected as much to celebrate the Earl's own valour in the fight as the loyal service of his men.

Highland society was patriarchal. A kinship bond, real or imagined, existed between clansfolk and their chief. The land was held in common. It was a primitive society that seemed to function with values and traditions which had been tried and tested. It lasted long and well perhaps because it had much worth if it did not have great riches.

Loyalty, honour and duty linked men to chief. They would faithfully fight and bravely die for their chief. His enemies were their enemies. The spoils of war were shared even if the glory went to the chief.

Feuding between the clans was for many centuries the Highland way of life – William, the Fifth Earl, died as a result of Mackay vengeance. His brother had killed a Chief of Mackay and Mackays were unwilling to forgive and forget. For 400 years the two families had a bitter feud.

According to Sheila Forman, a writer whose delightful articles on Scottish country houses long graced the glossy Scottish monthly magazines, "the first time Dunrobin Castle is mentioned by name is in a charter dated 1401 to which Robert, 6th Earl put his seal" (Forman, 1967,150). She suggests that "possibly the castle is named after this earl". On the other hand Earl Robert (or Robin) may simply have been responsible for the rebuilding or enlarging of an earlier castle as parts of Dunrobin reputedly date back to the late thirteenth century. The iron yett or gate of the supposedly 1401 tower is still preserved in the castle. By its name however Earl Robin seems to have got the credit for building it but we may never be sure exactly what he built. Groome is certainly dismissive of him stating that of Earl Robert "history knows absolutely nothing" (Groome, 1885, II, 445). While it is refreshing to see an historian being so honest, in this case it is not strictly true, for we do know that Robert had married the daughter of King Robert II's infamous brother, Alexander, who rejoiced in the magnificent yet blood curdling name of the 'Wolf of Badenoch'.

The line which could be traced back to Freskin came to a rather unbecoming end. John, the 8th Earl, went mad and while he was regarded as being unfit to manage his affairs this had not deterred him from marrying and siring children. Weakness in the head did not mean that other parts of the anatomy did not function perfectly! His son and heir inherited all his father's incapabilities and none of his mother's abilities whereas his sister seems to have obtained them in abundance in the reverse order. Miss Forman has told of the delightful old account of the pair – the 9th Earl "was weak of judgement, deprived of naturall wit and understanding, being able to govern neither himself nor others; bot his sister Lady Elizabeth Sutherland (the wyff of Adam Gordon of Aboyne) was full of spirite and witt" (Forman, 1967, 150).

The 9th Earl, unmarried and imbalanced, had been placed in his sister's care and she had assumed the role of Mistress of Dunrobin and on his death claimed the Earldom for herself.

Her half-brother, Alexander Sutherland, the rightful heir, put up a gallant struggle and although he had captured the castle was forced to surrender it to a greater force of Gordons. The fighting continued for about another year but when Alexander was killed in a skirmish all hopes of unseating the pretendress ended. As an example to all "his head wes careid to Dunrobin on a spear, and wes placed vpon the height of the great tour" (Moncrieffe, 1982, 22 – 7). It was sufficient deterrent – no one rose against the Mistress.

Elizabeth was, after lengthy legal proceedings, confirmed as Countess of Sutherland in her own right and her historians have been generous to her, – one thought her "of good judgement and great modestie" but we might add 'of great cunning and much duplicitie'. With the advent of Mrs Gordon to the earldom there was to begin a line of Gordon, Earls of Sutherland. She was in turn succeeded by her grandson, the 11th Earl, who in spite of being nicknamed 'Good Earl John' was not universally admired. In 1567 he and his wife were poisoned by his aunt, Isobel Sinclair, at Helmsdale Castle in an attempt to gain the earldom for her own son. Isobel Sinclair's evil scheme came to grief, however, for her son by some misfortune, got the poisoned cup intended for the future 12th Earl.

Initially everything did not quite go the new Earl's way. He was forced to marry the daughter of the Earl of Caithness but when he came of age he managed to obtain a divorce and was then able to marry the lady of his own choice, the divorced wife of the Earl of Bothwell who had by then become the third husband of Mary, Queen of Scots. There are few things as tortuous as the dynasties of great Scottish families!

The 14th Earl was a contemporary of James Graham, the man who would become the famous Marquis of Montrose. Both men were educated at the University of St Andrews and both were signatories to the National Covenant of 1638 which condemned the King's interference in ecclesiastical affairs. The 14th Earl and Montrose were soon to be on opposing sides in the Covenanting struggles of the first half of the seventeenth century. The 14th Earl was too late to participate in the Battle of Dunbar but he was probably the key figure in creating the Baronial mansion house at Dunrobin which can still be discerned amid all the later additions. His initials and those of his Countess can be seen on the pediments of the windows of the part which they had built.

It was the 16th Earl who revived the Sutherland surname in place of that of Gordon. He had been strongly opposed to the Jacobites and helped bring about their defeat in 1715. During Prince Charles' later attempts to regain the throne for the Stuart cause, the House of Sutherland was again firmly on the Hanoverian side. Although the castle was briefly held by the Jacobites and the Countess held captive the Earl managed to escape. The Jacobites who had taken the castle had been led by George, 3rd Earl of Cromartie, and when the Sutherlands had retaken Dunrobin the room in which Cromartie was captured was re-named the 'Cromartie Room' in honour of their celebrated prisoner. Sir Ian Moncreiffe has written: "Dunrobin was thus the last castle in Britain to be captured with bloodshed in time of war, and it seems fitting that its final captors were the Sutherlands themselves" (Moncrieffe, 1982, 227). It is also ironic because the Earl of Cromartie who was to forfeit his honours and his estates due to his support for the Jacobite cause was, perhaps as a near neighbour, leniently dealt with by the Earl of Sutherland. Although he was taken to Inverness and thence to the Tower in London and there tried for high treason and found guilty he was later granted remission for his life.

The family of the Earl of Cromartie were, in time, to regain their lands and supremely loyal service to a Hanoverian monarch ensured that even the title was restored in due course. The Cromarties, as we shall discover, were to have a major role to play in another and later episode of our story.

With defeat at Culloden the Jacobite cause floundered and fell. Red coats of the Hanoverian army and harsh Governmental policy ensured that the Stuarts would never again raise a Highland army and that peace would be maintained by force. The Sutherland family no longer needed to wage war to secure their future but legal battles would require to take the place of bloody ones.

Familial intrigues were not to pass with the collapse of the Jacobite hopes. Peace has problems no less real than those of war.

CHAPTER TWO

The Many Houses of
Leveson-Gower

Even great Scottish families have links over the Border. One such link is with the Gower family and with Stittenham in the North Riding of Yorkshire.

Stittenham may never have amounted to very much and although the ancient manor house has long gone the name of Gower Hall Farm still transports us back to mediaeval England and links with our tale. It is a real signpost to the past.

By the early twelfth century the surname Gower had a fairly wide geographical spread and no doubt there was once a connection with the Gower peninsula in South Wales. Here, however, let us limit our interest to the one branch of the family which had a connection with Stittenham.

The origin of the name appears to be from the Norman le Goher or de Guher and the family's land holding may have been a result of the Norman conquest. By the end of the thirteenth century one John Gower was lord of the manor and styled himself 'of Stittenham'.

From the earliest times the Gower family seemed to have been one of some significance – in art and letters as well as and more particularly in affairs of state. Lawrence Gower was

29

involved in the capture and execution of the King Edward II's controversial, frivolous and influential favourite, Piers Gaveston, the Earl of Cornwall – regarded by many as a threat to the power of the Lords and by the Queen as a rival in the King's affections.

It was long acclaimed that the fourteenth-century poet John Gower was linked to the Stittenham family and was supposedly born there in 1320. In the middle of the nineteenth century one of the farms at Stittenham was referred to as Gore Close Farm which is an interesting fact for our Gower family always seem to have pronounced their name as GORE rhyming with core (as in apple) whereas the poet Gower seems to have rhymed his name with 'power' (as in control).

The Gowers seem to have long served the crown even when it was not safe to do so. Sir John Gower – standard-bearer to Prince Edward, King Henry VI's son – was beheaded after the crushing Lancastrian defeat at Tewkesbury in 1471, one of the key battles of the Wars of the Roses. Another John Gower met his death, fighting for King Henry VIII, on the field at Flodden in 1513 when the Scots lost both the battle and their king. The noted sixteenth-century artist George Gower, the grandson of Sir John Gower of Stittenham, became the court painter to Queen Elizabeth I.

Sir Thomas Gower was to become Captain of the little Scottish Border town of Eyemouth as well as Marshal of Berwick. He supervised the construction of much of the town's fortifications which were to be an effective defence system against Scottish attack and helped make Berwick one of the outstanding fortified towns in Europe. When the Lord Protector the Duke of Somerset invaded Scotland in his attempt at the 'rough wooing' of Mary, Queen of Scots, Gower led a troop of horsemen and fought on the field at the Battle of Pinkie near Musselburgh. Although the English were to achieve a spectacular victory Gower was taken prisoner and was only released on the payment of a hefty ransom. He then continued to advise other northern towns on fortifications and on a later visit to Scotland, as master of ordnance of the army sent to besiege the port of Leith, he proved that he was as good at bringing down fortifications as he was at putting them up.

A baronetcy was conferred on Sir Thomas Gower in 1620 and the family were to remain the most loyal of supporters of the crown throughout the troubled years of the seventeenth century and even during the torment of the English Civil War.

With the second baronet there was the first of a succession of marriages which not only brought the Gowers doubtlessly fine wives but the prospects of healthy inheritances and spectacular estates, Sir Thomas Gower had married Frances Leveson, daughter of Sir Richard Leveson. If it was not a marriage made in heaven it was certainly one with much material earthly value. It transformed fairly simple country squires into landed magnates.

Although they were to long remain Lords of the Manor at Stittenham, with an estate of some 1,300 or so acres, their real landed interests were soon to move westward and be concentrated in broad acres in Staffordshire and Shropshire.

The Gowers had arrived.

Let us now turn to the Levesons, a family of some fame and not a little fortune.

The name Leveson, supposedly meaning 'beloved son', was a singularly appropriate one for they seem to have been favourably treated by fate. Occasionally the name was written as Luson, which is understandable as it seems to have been pronounced like loosen (as in slacken). Its frequent mispelling over the years as 'Leverson' comes close to a reasonable, common-sense pronunciation of the name.

The particular branch which concerns our tale settled at Willenhall, near Wolverhampton, and in 1274 acquired the manor of Wolverhampton by the marriage of Edward Leveson with the heiress.

The growth of urban centres meant the rise of a mercantile élite to service the needs of the increasing populations of these towns. The Levesons were such a family and as wool-merchants they prospered and with their wealth sought to

acquire more and more property. James Leveson had determined to turn town merchants into country squires. With
available land in short supply it seemed as though his high
hopes might early flounder but the hand of fate, in the guise
of King Henry VIII's religious policies, came into play and the
Levesons were considerable buyers of monastic buildings
following their dissolution. James Leveson purchased
Lilleshall Abbey and its lands in Shropshire and the Trentham
Abbey estate in Staffordshire, and speedily began to disman-
tle them to ensure that if there was to be a reversal in official
policy the buildings would be impossible to restore. When his
wife died he married the widow of wealthy ironmonger,
Thomas Michell. Michell was reputed to be one of the richest
commoners in London and when he died his wife was left a
considerable fortune. The Levesons had therefore married
well and inherited another convenient fortune. It is worth
noting the source of the treasure for the name Michell will
surprisingly figure again in our tale.

Leveson's great-grandson in time inherited the estates and
Admiral Sir Richard Leveson's statue can be seen in a niche at
Trentham to this day. He had a distinguished naval career
and spent much of his short life in the seemingly never
ending quest to destroy Spain as the rival naval power. Sir
Richard's nephew and heir, also a Sir Richard, had a new
Elizabethan-style mansion built at Trentham in 1634. He was
a true Royalist and to publicly declare the point had wooden
panels bearing the Royal Arms of Charles I placed in the
churches at Trentham and Lilleshall. He also suffered for his
support of the king and even his new home was damaged by
Cromwell's forces. The panels still hang in these two churches
and remain a testimony to his loyalty but holes in the panel at
Trentham Church made by Cromwellian bullets prove that
supporting the wrong side in a Civil War can be a dangerous
game.

There is a story about Lady Katherine Leveson, Sir
Richard's widow. When she died in 1674 her will revealed her
wishes –

I, Katherine Leveson, do bequeath my body to be buried in Lilleshall Church, by the monument where my dear husband lies. To the Minister of Trentham whom I desire to bury me, I give twenty pounds and a mourning gown for his pains. And to the Minister of Lilleshall I give five pounds to let the other bury me; or else I give nothing, in case he be against it (*Lilleshall Church Guide*).

One hopes the Lilleshall minister saw sense and allowed the other to conduct the service.

It was the heiress to the Trentham and Lilleshall estates, Frances Leveson, who married Sir Thomas Gower of Stittenham. Their son adopted the surname Leveson-Gower for he became the embodiment of the two great familial strands we have briefly examined and Sir William Leveson-Gower inherited the Lilleshall and Trentham estates as well as the manor of Stittenham but he was not one to rest on his laurels for he too married well – he wed Lady Jane Grenville, daughter of the Earl of Bath.

The Grenvilles were an old English family and among their number had been Sir Roger Grenville who drowned with the sinking of Henry VIII's flagship *Mary Rose* in 1545. Another distinguished member of the family was the naval commander Sir Richard Grenville whose command of the *Revenge* became a legendary chapter in the war with Spain. Lord Tennyson described Grenville's heroic activities in his ballad 'The Revenge'. Lady Jane's grandfather had been the popular Royalist officer Sir Bevil Grenville who fell in the Royalist victory at Lansdown Hill, near Bath in 1643.

Although 'Grenville' did not become an additional surname of our family one of Lady Jane's great-grandsons was to become ennobled as Earl Granville and thus began another aristocratic branch of the family. One of the Earl's daughters was the now forgotten novelist Lady Georgina Fullarton, one of whose unread books bears the delightful title *Too Strange not to be True*. Undoubtedly the most distinguished member of that branch was the 2nd Earl, a great Victorian statesman and eminent Foreign Secretary.

Sir William Leveson-Gower did not attain any great offices of state but diligently for more than thirty years served as Member of Parliament for Newcastle-under-Lyme. John, the eldest son of Sir William and Lady Jane, married the daughter of the Duke of Rutland and after making his mark as a Member of Parliament for his father's old seat, was elevated to the peerage as Baron Gower of Stittenham. He was one of the commissioners who concluded the Treaty of Union between Scotland and England of 1707.

His son also had a notable public career becoming a distinguished Lord Justice of England and also served as Lord Privy Seal. With the advent of Bonnie Prince Charles and the Jacobite Rising to attempt to regain the throne for the Stuarts Lord Gower was able to overlook his earlier flirtation with the Jacobite cause and raised a regiment of foot to aid the Hanoverian monarchy. With the successful repression of the Jacobites although without much help from Gower's forces the gesture of loyalty from Gower was suitably rewarded – he was created Viscount Trentham and Earl Gower. It has always paid to be on the winning side!

Disraeli in his novel *Lothair*, in a rather thinly veiled disguise, described the Leveson-Gowers thus –

> . . . a family with charm that always attracted and absorbed heiressess . . . beautiful women who generation after generation brought their bright castles and their broad manors to swell the state and rent rolls of the family . . . (Stuart,1982, 30).

As we have seen, it was long thus, for the family seemed to be ever upwardly mobile but if anyone could truly be entitled to claim the distinction of putting the family on the map it was the Earl's son, Granville. He not only married Lady Louisa Egerton, eldest daughter of the immensely rich Duke of Bridgewater (the Canal Duke – 'father of British inland navigation') and thereby succeeded to a fortune but was to become the 1st Marquis of Stafford and a Knight of the Garter.

He too served as Lord Privy Seal and held various other cabinet posts including Lord President of the Council. He was also one of the few men to have actually turned down the opportunity to be Prime Minister.

'Egerton' was also not destined to become an additional surname but a later younger son was to adopt it as his surname and that branch prospered as the Earls of Ellesmere.

Granville, the 1st Marquis of Stafford, was also a great builder. He employed Sir William Chambers, the great neo-classical architect, to design Gower House in Whitehall – now gone – which was long regarded as being one of the most beautiful houses in London. Henry Holland and Capability Brown were employed to transform Trentham and its parkland. There had been much building and rebuilding at Trentham as each new heir succeeded to the estate and left his mark on it by endeavouring to make the house into his very own home. Where the others had created fine houses the 1st Marquis had created a palatial mansion, almost as grand as Buckingham Palace. The family had become, all but in name, truly princes.

By the late eighteenth century the family of Leveson-Gower had therefore acquired an impressive string of titles, vast wealth, some magnificent houses and extensive estates as well as a host of lesser properties. Viscount Trentham, the eldest son of the 1st Marquis of Stafford, was thus a most eligible young bachelor. But who on earth could be a suitable partner for such a young man? A princess? An heiress?

CHAPTER THREE

Happy Union – Unhappy Events

With a smile on her lips, and a tear in her eye.
SIR WALTER SCOTT – from *Marmion*

The walls of many old churches are cluttered with commemorative tablets. Dornoch Cathedral has only a sprinkling of them: in the chancel there is a particularly handsome classical memorial which commemorates William 17th Earl of Sutherland and his wife. The story behind the monument must surely be among the saddest in the annals of any of the great landed families.

It seems that the Earl had been playing with his infant daughter, Catherine, in Dunrobin Castle when he dropped the child. She struck her head upon the hearth and died as a result of the accident. Heartbroken, the young couple took their younger daughter, Elizabeth, to her maternal grandmother, Lady Alva, in Edinburgh while they went off on holiday to escape the scene of the tragedy and to console themselves in their tragic loss. They went to the fashionable city of Bath but there the Earl contracted a fever and as his wife nursed him night and day she became so weak that she too caught the infectious disease. She died on 1 June 1766 and her husband gave out only two weeks later. They were both laid to rest at Holyrood Abbey on 9 August 1766.

Thus it came about that a little girl, barely one year of age, succeeded to the titles and estates of Sutherland. Although she was the rightful heir, male relatives such as Sir Robert Gordon of Gordonstoun and George Sutherland of Forse claimed the title. They had perhaps overlooked the fact that a precedent had been established when, in 1514, an earlier Elizabeth had succeeded on the death of her brother. There was much at stake so there was considerable litigation and the famously long and costly legal dispute of 'The Sutherland Peerage Case' only came to its just conclusion when the House of Lords in 1771 decided in favour of Elizabeth. There seems to have been much rejoicing when the result was known – bonfires were lit on the estates owned by her wards and friends while a great party was held in Sutherland. Later the factor or estate manager was presented with a large bill for the "whisky and other drink, bread and cheese, powder and shot, consumed by above 500 of the Countess' tenants who had met in Golspy to rejoice in her carrying the peerage" (Forman, 1967, 151).

She was not only titled and popular but had inherited the largest estate in the land. She was thus a most eligible young lady. Lord Byron was later to conclude that she was not only beautiful but that "her manners were princessly" (Fraser, 1892, 495).

Who was to marry such a princess?

The late eighteenth century was a time of twin evils for Highland society. It was a time when what had been considered to be clan lands became simply the lands of the clan chief and also an age when many Highland landlords and clan chiefs became increasingly absent. Rather than spend time among their more lowly kinsmen they sought the company of their equals and enjoyed the social whirls of Edinburgh and London. They had to squeeze their rentrolls in order to finance the increasing expenditure on the conspicuous consumption required to look and act the part in the capitals. It became a necessary and component part of being a Highland Chief that one had to spend so much money and have such a good time in London.

It was perhaps not in the least surprising that a young girl of wealth and status should wish to be in London and to savour the delights of its social scene. In 1779 the teenage Countess embarked on "a prolonged stay" (Fraser, 1892, 467) in London with the principal objects being the completion of her education in the social mores of the times and her acceptance by London society. While in London she seemingly had her first portrait painted by one of the rising artistic stars, Alan Ramsay's pupil, Sir George Chalmers.

After a brief spell in Scotland where she had begun to interest herself in her estates and had made some suggestions as to their administration she again returned south, alternating between Edinburgh and London. It was while in London that she met the shy young George Granville Leveson-Gower, Viscount Trentham and eldest son of rich and landed Earl Gower.

Trentham had been a rather sickly youth with poor eyesight and this had encouraged an academic bent and studious look. He had gone up to Christ Church, Oxford before embarking on his 'Grand Tour' of Europe as all young men of refinement and breeding were wont to do. He, too, was elected to the Commons as representative for the old family seat of Newcastle-under-Lyme although he was later to become MP for the county of Stafford.

The Leveson-Gowers had long had a history of successful and highly profitable matchmaking but now they were to exceed what was an already mightily impressive record.

In 4 September 1785, at the age of twenty-one, Elizabeth Gordon, Countess of Sutherland in her own right, married Viscount Trentham. Within a year the old Earl was elevated up the aristocratic ladder to become the 1st Marquis of Stafford and the young couple became the Earl and Countess Gower.

For the next few years they turned their attention to Dunrobin and "at considerable expense" (Fraser, 1892, 470) began to transform the place into a more worthy and noble family seat. Scotland was not, of course, to consume all their interest. In 1787 they visited Italy and while in Rome they called on the British Ambassador who informed the Countess that if she watched from a particular window at a specific time she might see the legendary Prince Charles Edward

Stuart pass by. She eagerly waited but instead of a charismatic Bonnie Prince Charlie she saw "an old infirm broken down man" (Fraser, 1892, 472) for the tragic, if romantic, figure of the 1745 Jacobite Rising had by then become a sad relic of a bygone age and indeed was to die in January 1788 with all the hopes of his youth buried forever. The Countess had glimpsed a piece of history but she herself was to sample a piece of excitement in what was to become one of the greatest historical landmarks of all time.

In 1790, somewhat surprisingly, since he had had no previous diplomatic experience even if a fluent French speaker, Gower was appointed British Ambassador to Paris. It was a post of great importance and came at a time of great significance, not only for France but for the rest of Europe. France was then in the full flood of Revolution. The Marquis had pleaded with his son not to accept the post but Gower had been determined and shortly after their arrival in Paris wrote to say that they would not only "brave the tempest" but that they were preparing their home for their children and, indeed, soon the two children joined them. The Countess was to become a close friend of Marie Antoinette, the wife of Louis XVI, and their eldest son became a playmate of the Dauphin. Lady Gower helped the Royal Family escape from the Tuilleries for she had smuggled clothes to them which allowed them to flee in disguise. The Queen made her escape dressed in Lady Gower's clothes, the young Dauphin in Viscount Trentham's and, if we are to believe the story, the King was dressed as a page. It is perhaps little wonder that the flight ended in failure and the family was captured and returned to Paris.

In order to protect their house from the angry mob the Gowers found it necessary to have boldly chalked upon its doors 'Ambassade d'Angleterre' in an attempt to give it some diplomatic immunity for it had become perhaps just too exciting a time to be in Paris. The days of strained amity between Britain and France, however, soon reached breaking point and in 1792 diplomatic relations between Britain and

Revolutionary France were broken off. The Ambassador was recalled to England and the family hastily gathered their belongings and headed for the Channel but were arrested and brought before the revolutionary tribunal at Abbeville. After some anxiety and a little detention they were permitted to leave and make their way to the coast and to safety.

A later member of the Sutherland lineage has informed us that he had a diamond necklace which had once belonged to Marie Antoinette and which rejoiced in the name of the 'Collet de la Reine' as well as two magnificent gilt armchairs with the initials, 'M.A.' interlaced on their backs. These had come from the Queen's summerhouse, the Petit Trianon, and were, no doubt, acquired not simply because of a developing love for things French but kept as mementoes of these dramatic days in Paris.

After the guillotining of Louis XVI the Countess was quick to raise a regiment of Fencibles in Sutherland. She had witnessed, at first hand, the horrors of revolution and wished to secure a more peaceful future for her family and for her ways.

While they were absent their Highland estate had its own little bit of excitement. In 1790 General James Grant, one of the trustees of the estate during her minority and a devoted friend, had to inform her that "owing to some careless neglect on the part of the carpenter the stables at Dunrobin were burned" (*Scotsman*, 14 June 1915). He also expressed his anxiety about the castle itself for he had been advised that others "did not think the castle safe under the care of the housekeeper, as she is apt, in her present solitude, to take a cup of comfort too freely" (Fraser, 1892) and thus advised the Countess to take out insurance cover for the castle. It was sound advice as fire was later to destroy much of the castle and its contents.

General Grant had fought during the American War of Independence and had been the first Governor of Florida during its brief spell as a British colony. His own castle of Ballindalloch had been burned by the Marquis of Montrose's forces in February 1645 so Grant well knew the damage fire could do to property whether the result of carelessness or wilful fire-raising.

On his return to England several government posts were offered to Lord Gower – Lord Steward and the Lieutenancy of Ireland – but, considering his eyesight to be too weak, he had declined to accept them. He was of such a frail and nervous disposition with such failing eyesight that, it is said, doctors advised him to refrain from having conjugal intercourse with his wife. Malicious rumours became rife that the Countess had several 'liaisons dangereuses' and that others had sired his children during Gower's enforced periods of celibacy. But that, as they say, is another story.

The Countess was a woman of considerable beauty and her passport painted a vivid picture of a not unattractive young lady – five foot tall, hair and eyebrows of light chestnut, eyes of dark chestnut, nose well formed, mouth small, chin round, forehead low and with a somewhat long face. The portrait of her by the fashionable portrait painter, John Hoppner, which still hangs in Dunrobin is an endearing and enduring likeness of a beautiful woman. It is little wonder that she had a string of admirers.

Certainly the Countess became one of the leading hostesses of her day and was able to flaunt her charm, wealth and status on a grand scale. She did not neglect her children and devoted much time to rearing her two boys and two girls. In her quieter moments she indulged in a little sketching and painting in water colours and she rather enjoyed partaking of snuff. She also corresponded regularly with Sir Walter Scott and both seem to have had a warm affection for each other and certainly both shared a romantic view of Scottish history.

In 1799 Lord Gower accepted the post of Postmaster General and for eleven years retained that office and during the period was rewarded with the Garter. In 1803, on his father's death, he succeeded as Marquis of Stafford and gained all the family properties of Stittenham, Trentham and Lilleshall. Earlier that year he had also inherited a windfall from the estate of his fabulously rich uncle, the Duke of Bridgewater. He was no longer a man of expectations: he had truly arrived. He had become, as the chronicler of the times had noted, a veritable 'leviathan of wealth'.

The original design of York House had been by Robert Smirke (later famed as architect of the British Museum) but after his quarrel with the 'grand old' Duke of York the work was entrusted to Benjamin Wyatt. When the Duke died, leaving a mountain of debts and the house unfinished, the government purchased the property and then leased it to the Marquis of Stafford who renamed it Stafford House. A pleasant two-storey house on a prime site in London it reflected the status of its new owner. It simply required to be transformed from house into palace and that was something the fortunes of the Staffords could with consummate ease realise.

Having largely retired from active politics the Marquis of Stafford increasingly devoted his time to patronage of the arts and improvements to his huge estates. Bridgewater House was extended and the public was given access to view his growing art collections. At Trentham new rooms were added and a splendid mausoleum built, but increasingly his sights focused – if that is the right word, given his long problem, – on his wife's vast acres in Sutherland. His knowledge of Scotland was somewhat limited. In his bachelor days he had once visited it and soon after their marriage he had attempted to make Dunrobin a more suitable and more modern home for an English aristocrat but essentially it had been left alone. Now there were to be long annual visits. In the past, Scotland had simply been a place in which to holiday but now Sutherland was to benefit from his organising and modernising zeal. It was almost bound to be a recipe for disaster.

CHAPTER FOUR

New Economics, New Dukedom
& New Houses

Old times were changed, old manners gone.
SIR WALTER SCOTT – from *The Lay of the Last Minstrel*

The Countess of Sutherland had adored her husband and her way of coming to terms with his death was to erect great statues and monuments – on a hill near Trentham, on a hillock at Lilleshall, on Ben Bhraggie, and in every church possible, including Dornoch Cathedral.

These monuments express in glowing sentiments the pious views of his widow and sycophantic utterances of his kinsmen as well as reflecting the values of the social élites of the day but the great man had not been universally admired. Indeed what he had done and what he represented was anathema to many people. To this day the Highland Clearances remain a highly emotive issue and nowhere more so than in Sutherland.

In June 1992 Golspie Gala Committee refused to floodlight the magnificent statue on Ben Bhraggie because of the policies carried out in the name of the 1st Duke of Sutherland, for he was held to be responsible for 'clearances' by which people in the straths of Sutherland were forced out to make room for sheep. Early in 1994 a Regional Councillor suggested that the statue be demolished and the resultant rubble be used to help repair the sea wall at Dunrobin. The Sutherland family had sought financial assistance towards the repairs and were thus compelled to seek funding elsewhere. Old animosities linger on. The Duke has not been forgotten or forgiven. The Sutherland Clearances have been well documented and we need not dwell on them here. The Duke had been attempting social engineering on a grand scale – moving people to where he wanted them and not where they wanted to be. He was attempting to make economic sense out of his estates and he spent a fortune trying to make the estates productive and make them pay. It has been a perennial Highland problem.

As the Highlands struggled to modernise in an age without constant battle, what had been believed to be commonly held clan lands became simply and legally (if rather euphemistically) converted into the personal property of the Clan Chief. The Clan Chief now increasingly saw himself as more of a lord over acres rather than chief over warriors. Centuries of loyal and devoted service of men for chief counted naught. Honour and respect given by countless generations of clans folk to the patriarchal leaders of Highland society merited little reward in the new economic order. Progress and profit became the buzz words of the age. Old ways were out: new ways were in. Traditional values and ties were severed. The future lay in sheep not swords. Men were needed to make prosperity for Dukes not to make war for chieftains. (The worth of the fighting qualities of clansmen long continued. Warriors would still be required and as soldiers in the British Army and in its regiments Highlanders have ever loyally served).

The Highlanders had lived in a feudal backwater – now they were to be hauled screaming into the modern world. Little or scant regard was to be paid to their wishes and aspirations. Southern economics and landlords' needs, real or imagined, became the cruel realities. Modernisation was to be a painful process, not a recipe for unmitigated joy.

In the eighteenth and nineteenth centuries Highland landlords attempted all of a limited range of options in an effort to make their estates pay. Black cattle, herring fishing, kelp gathering and sheep rearing were tried and found wanting and in the end deer forestry was the last rather pathetic hope. In our day Highland & Islands Development Boards and a sprinkling of industrialists have tried a different but still very limited range of newer options in attempting to create growth points – an atomic energy reactor here, aluminium smelting plants there, a pulp mill somewhere and oil rig production yards somewhere else. All were seen as keys to growth. The riches have remained elusive. All have been either near disastrous or at best had very limited success and the only continuing successes have been forestry, fish farming, hydro electricity production, and tourism. The success of these is welcome but success remains a fickle perception.

The picturesque ruins of Spinningdale are symbolic of the attempts to industrialise in the past. Some of the great industrialists of the day built these mills but scarcity of suitable labour and being so far from markets and supplies meant unviability or at least a comparative disadvantage as compared to other producers in the marketplace. Spinningdale looks forlornly south across the Dornoch Firth – far to the south lay the markets, the raw material and workforce.

Moving people from their homes might make economic sense but it is scarcely an act meriting much thanks from those evicted. The Duke callously served his own interests and they ran counter to the interests of his people. The estates in Hugh Miller's immortal words were "improved into a desert". Eviction is eviction no matter how prettily or progressive we might make it sound. The policies have had their defenders (few) and their detractors (many) so we need not elaborate on them here. Economics may be about guns and butter and tend to forget human feelings but this is a story about people and thus we cannot be dispassionate.

The Marquis of Stafford rationally, if cruelly, tried to exploit the resources of his domain. There were few who benefited. Few appreciated these efforts. One endeavour has, however, proved of lasting worth. In 1819, to legitimise whisky-distilling and utilise local barley, he built a distillery at Brora and a distillery in one shape or another has continued to this day.

Clynelish is one of the most delightful of peaty malts and is perhaps his only enduring contribution to economic development in Sutherland and it is certainly one which has given lasting pleasure to those who appreciate good whisky.

On 28 January 1833 the Marquis of Stafford was created Duke of Sutherland. While it was claimed that he had accepted that particular title in honour of his wife she was supposedly unhappy with the choice of name and desired somewhat haughtily to be known henceforth as the Duchess-Countess of Sutherland. The Duke did not live long to enjoy his new title and died later that year. His son therefore inherited the new dukedom while his widow remained, as she had always been, the Countess of Sutherland in her own right.

The 2nd Duke does not seem to have shared his father's modernising zeal and seemed to have been more willing to simply consolidate rather than reshape. He is a rather shadowy figure for he always seems to have been in the shade of his father and was later to be eclipsed by his dynamic son. He also seems to have been dominated by his wife.

Having fallen hopelessly in love with the unattainable Queen Louisa of Prussia, George Granville, Earl Gower vowed that he would never marry. At the age of thirty-seven however he had a change of heart and wed his seventeen year-old cousin, the vivacious Lady Harriet Howard, one of the daughters of the 6th Earl of Carlisle. Like all earlier Leveson-Gower matches this was also to prove a most fortunate marriage, not necessarily because of any great dowry she might bring or for her propensity for childbearing, but due to her extraordinary talent. With the splendours of Castle Howard as her home and reference point it was perhaps not surprising that great buildings and landscaped gardens should be her forte. In the fields of architecture and horticulture she was to become "a leader of the world of taste and fashion" (*The Times*, 28 October 1868). On the Marquis's choice of partner it had been assessed well when it was noted that "she proved to be an exciting if expensive choice" (Stuart, 1982, 32). She dragged her near lifeless husband into social activity and goaded him into action over his properties. She and her husband together transformed all the ducal houses. It is no exaggeration to state that while he might have inherited fine houses and grand gardens what they were to bequeath to future generations were masterworks.

They began married life in a house in London's Hamilton Place with Lilleshall as their principal country seat. Lady Harriet rather disparagingly referred to that mansion as "the farm house" and compared to Castle Howard it lacked much. Soon Sir Jeffry Wyatville, then completing major works at Windsor Castle for King George IV, was called in. He created a fine stately white stone Tudor house of great dignity at a cost, believed to be around £80,000.

Harriet had very much approved of her father-in-law's acquisition of York House and delighted in the various works which transformed it into the more palatial Stafford House. When she and her husband acquired the house work did not cease and another £80,000 was estimated to be spent by the Staffords. Sir Charles Barry had been summoned to put the finishing touches to the interior and his work had met with much approval – the Great Gallery and Staircase Hall became two of the grandest spaces in England. It is perhaps little wonder that Queen Victoria was supposed to have said "I have come from my home to your palace". Stafford House was not simply to be a glittering display of wealth in itself but was to become one of the great social and political centres of Victorian London.

Perhaps because they had not been totally satisfied with the Wyatville efforts at Lilleshall Sir Charles Barry was the preferred choice when Trentham was to receive treatment on the death of the old Duke. Under Barry, Trentham became a magnificent Italianate palace engulfing the not inconsiderable house already on the site. Tall tower and stately rooms made Trentham the model to be emulated when others looked to build – Prince Albert too looked and admired and his Osborne House owed a little to his hours at Trentham.

What the landscape gardener John Claudius Loudon called

a "great dull flat place" was transformed by Barry and Nesfield into a magnificent formal garden which stepped down from the house by means of a succession of terraces towards the lake which Capability Brown had created. Now Barry had linked house to lake and at the end of the path placed a statue of Perseus while at the end of the distant vista was the statue of the 1st Duke. It was a garden of delight.

The Duke supposedly spent £125,000 on Trentham. Barry had carried out his improving works on almost every aspect of the property and even Trentham Church was rebuilt using stone from the former church.

In 1849, after only a few months in the ownership of the Sutherlands, another of his houses, Cliveden was completely destroyed by fire. An Italianate villa was placed on the founds of the old house and around the frieze in Latin there is, in Roman lettering, an inscription supposedly composed by Gladstone that Barry had built this with "skill and devotion". No one could deny it.

When they inherited Dunrobin it had already become a house which had developed and grown in haphazard fashion into a mighty baronial castle. With the aid of Barry and local architect William Leslie, and not a little advice from James Loch, the notorious if efficient estate agent, Dunrobin became a grandiose French château. The castle trebled in size with a host of rooms to house a vast extended family and a suite of Royal apartments for Victoria and her Consort to share in the Scottish experience. Magnificent new rooms looked down over new formal gardens of sheer splendour. Such enchantment did not come cheaply – it is thought that £60,000 was spent on the creation of this new Dunrobin.

Of her spendthrift ways one of her granddaughters was later to recall

> My grandmother had always a soul above finance, and as her Cloud Castle grew beneath the designs of Barry she had him constantly in consultation, both north and south. Naturally, an architect's time is money and where she thought he was a guest, his view was more

professional. When the bill came in she was staggered at the figures. The story goes that my grandfather recognising her genius for building, looked indulgently on what it had cost and paid the bill cheerfully. (Balfour,1930, 221).

It was perhaps little wonder that their agent, James Loch, should have repeatedly called for some financial retrenchment. At the rate money was being spent, the Leviathan of Wealth would soon be reduced to a bankrupt tadpole.

Barry had not been the only architect employed by the Sutherlands. The great rebuilding programme did not stop at the portico of the big house. Barry may have had the big houses but George Devey was to design many lesser buildings – farms, cottages and lodges for all the estates. The Sutherlands were to become his "most valuable clients" (Allibone, 1991, 50) and his buildings around Golspie still delight the eye.

Harriet had been Mistress of the Robes from more or less Victoria's succession until 1861 when both the Queen and Harriet became widows. For twenty-five years she was the friend and confidante of the Queen and shared all the intimate secrets of the Queen's life.

Harriet was active in attempts to reduce and abolish slavery worldwide. She was also noted for her philanthropic works at home and while she herself did much to aid the distressed poorer classes in London and elsewhere she was a fervent admirer and supporter of Lord Shaftesbury's good works concerning the plight of factory children. Shaftesbury was later to recall

> She has been to me in heart, in temper, in demeanor, the most uniformly kind, considerate and zealous ally and co-operator that ever lived . . . She was ever ready to give her palaces, her presence, and her ardent efforts for the promotion of anything that was generous and compassionate and good . . . (Sutherland, 1957, 36).

It was a glowing tribute to a lady, regarded as "one of the

most widely known and most widely popular members of the aristocracy" (*The Times*, 28 October 1868).

The 2nd Duke added the name Sutherland to the family surname. They had long been aristocratic and in a plutocratic age the quantity and quality of one's great houses mattered. The House of Sutherland had, with the aggrandisement of Dunrobin, obtained its great house.

The Duke and Duchess deserved to be remembered for with much taste and no shortage of funds they created great houses. A statue of the 2nd Duke was placed opposite the main gates to Dunrobin (at the little station at Dunrobin). Within the policies of Dunrobin an Eleanor type cross with a bronze bust under the canopy was erected to Harriet's memory. He had quietly paid for great houses and she had enthusiastically ensured that they were as great as possible.

The Duke's statue tells us his memory was "loved, revered and cherished". His are qualities which we cannot now gauge but the more modest scope of the two memorials, lacking the overpowering might of the Ben Bhraggie statue or the very public presence of the memorial fountain to the Duchess-Countess in the middle of Golspie, commemorate two more attractive people.

His son and heir, George Granville William, had, at the age of twenty, married his young neighbour, the attractive and charming Anne Hay Mackenzie, heiress of the Cromarty estates. When the 3rd Duke succeeded to the titles and estates on his father's death, Queen Victoria, due to her great fondness for the family and as a mark of personal esteem, restored the old earldom on his wife and she became the Countess of Cromartie in her own right. They were truly a family with everything – near countless acres, some of the grandest of houses and no shortage of titles. Who could ask for more?

Yet, more was indeed necessary. Satisfaction is an unsatisfactory state for those with health and wealth.

With any new Duke things were never likely to be static. With this particular new Duke action was to be the by-word. The pace of change to the ducal houses was however to ease with the arrival of the 3rd Duke – there was presumably not much left to do to them, they were near enough perfect. He had other interests and a more global perspective. Unlike his parents he wanted modernising changes made to the estates and not to the houses. Like his grandfather he was to be to an 'improving' landowner but with more winsome ways.

CHAPTER FIVE

Midst Dreaming Spires

But search the land of living men,
Where wilt thou find their like agen?
SIR WALTER SCOTT – from *Marmion*

Few families have double barrelled or even triple barrelled names like the Sutherland-Leveson-Gowers. The Michell family for all their more humble ways, were a far from uninteresting family.

Meaning 'son of Michael', Michell is a variant of the more common Mitchell. The urge to insert that 't' has obviously proved irresistible to many people and frequent references to our Michells have been so misspelt. Quite where the Michells originated from has been long forgotten but it is an Anglo-French name and it may also have come with the Conquest. The name has had long and frequent use but one branch of the Michell family has its roots in rural Devon and a blossoming in the Anglican Church and not a little involvement with the universities of Oxford and Cambridge.

In 1769 Rev. Edward Michell, born in Diptford in Devon, became Headmaster of King's School in Bruton and was to remain there for thirty years; much of it spent in long and bitter disputes with the Governors over the poverty-stricken appearance of the school, the state of repair of his house and not least his pay. He maintained they did little to help the school while they maintained he did nothing for his salary. Two nephews of the headmaster perhaps merit mention. Richard was to become a fellow of some distinction of Wadham College, Oxford while Edward, a solicitor in Bruton, was to have four sons, one of whom was another Richard Michell.

The younger Richard Michell became a brilliant student at Wadham College and then became a Fellow at Lincoln College where he was considered the most successful private tutor of his time. On marriage he was compelled to give up the tutorship and went to Magdalen Hall, firstly as its Vice Principal and later as its Principal. When Magdalen Hall was incorporated into a college – Hertford College – Michell was to become its first Principal. Hertford College had its origins in the thirteenth century but had been dissolved in 1805 and it was largely due to Michell's energetic efforts and widespread influence that the college had been refounded.

Oxford's colleges are nothing if not superb buildings and Hertford College, in spite of its fairly recent re-founding, has some of its finest college buildings. Almost all are the work of one architect – Thomas Graham Jackson – and many are built in what has been delightfully nicknamed as the Anglo-Jackson style. The Bridge of Sighs, linking the two parts of the college, was later gifted by Lady St Helier in memory of her husband who as Sir Francis Jeune had been a distinguished High Court Judge and for long President of the Probate and Divorce Division. He had been one of Michell's principal supporters in the Governing Body of the University and became one of the first Fellows of the new Hertford. On his death he left the college a legacy of £500 and his portrait hangs in the Old Hall. Jeune not only thus contributed much to Hertford but he would contribute more to the Michell saga in the years to come, though sadly in a less happy direction. That story, however, must wait.

Richard Michell held many university posts, including that of Professor of Logic but it was in his role as Public Orator at Oxford that his commanding presence gained a wider audience, even if his speeches, long renowned for their excellence, were largely wasted on an unappreciative, tumultuous rabble. It does not seem to have worried Michell, who simply carried on regardless. That he was generally a genial soul who "excelled in after-dinner oratory" (Pattison, 1885, 266) seems to have been the accepted view. Mark Pattison, later Principal of Lincoln College, has offered an alternative view in what has been called the "pungent pages" of his *Memoirs* Pattison, where he "mingled admiration with acrimony" (*The Times*, 15 November 1926) but a recent writer has shrewdly and sensbly concluded that Michell "distrusted and disliked Pattison; Pattison returned the compliment" (Green, in Pattison, 1988, 181).

Although Pattison has stated that Michell was a "disappointed man" who found himself simply "shelved" at Magdalen there would seem to be little or no evidence to sustain the view. Michell seems to have loved Magdalen Hall and it loved him. His proudest moment was to see it become a fully-fledged College. Hertford to this day remains his memorial. A portrait of Richard Michell was gifted by his eldest son and thus his genial face still looks down over new generations of students in the dining hall of Hertford College.

The family of Richard and Emily Michell were children of which any Victorian parents would be proud. The law and the church were to continue to be served but they were also to find new avenues as Imperial expansion offered new opportunities in which to make one's mark. Several of the children were good students who were to become good teachers but it was as much on the sports field as in the groves of academe that they were to excel.

Devotees of Rodgers and Hammerstein's wonderful *The King and I* will have a vivid recollection of Siam's attempts to modernise in the latter half of the nineteenth century. One of those involved in the modernising process even if not a character in the film was Richard and Emily's eldest son – Edward – for he was to become Legal Advisor to the King of Siam in 1885 with the chief object of introducing domestic reform.

Edward had also gone to Oxford where he had excelled (firsts in Classics and in Law and History) but he had also much success as a sportsman in the arena, river and track. He thus had amassed a fine collection of silverware in the shape of cups and trophies to prove his prowess as boxer, oarsman and athlete. He was also author of a popular handbook on boxing. One of his great moments of fame at university had been when he acquired the nickname 'Hungry Michell' after scoffing a record number of pancakes one Shrove Tuesday.

He was called to the Bar in 1869 but before going into practice studied at the University of Paris during that momentous year of 1870. He got caught up in the Siege of Paris and wrote a vivid account of his experiences, *Siege Life in Paris by One of the Besieged* (1878). On his return to Oxford he became Lecturer in Law at Hertford College and also edited a collection of his father's orations. Among his interests were falconry and drama. He wrote a book on the former and, according to the eminent literary critic, George Saintsbury, he "supplied the living centre piece to Irving's production of Tennyson's play" (Becket) as performed at Windsor in 1893.

The second son, Richard, also embarked upon a legal career and rose to become Professor of Law at Presidency College, Madras, one of India's premier educational establishments. He became a High Court Judge in Madras in 1899.

Though the Michell family did not produce a governess, they did provide a near equivalent, for Roland Michell was for a time in charge of Prince Ibrahim Pasha, the son of the Khedive of Egypt. He later became resident Commissioner, at Limassol in the island of Cyprus. On his retiral in 1911, and as part of King George's Coronation Honours List, Michell was made a Companion of the Order of St Michael and St George (CMG).

Arthur was the only son to follow in his father's footsteps by becoming a cleric. In 1891 he became Vicar of St Mary's Church Sheriffhales, in Shropshire, where the Duke of Sutherland was patron of the living. St Mary's is a pretty little church with parts dating back to the thirteenth century but much also dating from the seventeenth century when, after receiving severe damage during the Civil War it was restored. Pillars and arches removed from the ruins of nearby Lilleshall Abbey were then incorporated into its structure. Arthur was to remain at St Mary's until his retiral in 1922.

The fourth son, Herbert, graduated from the new Hertford College and seems to have remained in Oxford and married his cousin Harriett, daughter of William Blair, who had long served in the East India Company Civil Service.

The baby of the family was Walter and although not a distinguished student at Cambridge he excelled in sports and played in the first recognised inter-university Rugby match. He also rowed for Cambridge against his brothers' university. Walter had a long association with Rugby School where he was a master and house master before briefly serving as Assistant Head Master and latterly as a Trustee of the School, representing the masters on the governing body. He was a much liked master and although he was not considered a great teacher, it was noted that Walter was

> a man of buoyant disposition and wide sympathies and who loved to do generous things in a large-hearted and casual way. In this cheerful presence lame dogs ceased to notice the stiles and came to believe that all their legs were sound (The Times, 16 December 1925).

That must surely be the mark of a truly great teacher and of a remarkably nice man.

There were two Michell daughters of which the elder, Elizabeth, married James Thornton Hoskins, a one-time student at Oxford. She seems to have led an uneventful life as wife and mother of two daughters and two sons. The younger daughter was to marry her cousin Arthur Kindersley Blair. Almost all of what follows is about the very eventful life of that remarkable woman.

The Michells were a gifted family whose gifts and talents enriched their own lives and times. They were a family who possessed much in a spiritual rather than temporal sense but it was Mary Caroline who was to prove the most successful in purely financial terms. Even she, however, commenced in a rather unpromising way by marrying that not very well-off former officer of the 71st Highlanders, but more of that later.

In 1931 when Roland Michell died he marked the passing of

an age. His generation of the Michells in their diverse ways had served their country and their society well even if their achievements were largely unsung and unhonoured. A lowly CMG had been the only official recognition of much effort, some notable success and even some substantial achievements. Their service and their talents had been rich but they had not been richly rewarded. Mary Caroline on the other hand was to achieve an abundance of riches and not a little fame.

CHAPTER SIX

Home and Away

Fair these broad meads, these hoary woods are grand;
But we are exiles from our father's land.
SIR WALTER SCOTT – from *Canadian Boat Song*
(disputed authorship).

Apart from the aristocratic Sutherland-Leveson-Gowers and the academic Michells, the third family which concerns our tale is that of Blair.

The name Blair seems to have its origins in the Scots Gaelic word 'blar' which may mean 'battlefield' or simply 'field'. Many of the place names which have Blair as a prefix seem to have had a relatively peaceful past, so the 'field' origin might be more accurate, if less dramatic.

Early examples of the use of the personal name Blair can be found sprinkled across Scotland. Many also moved south to seek their fortune and a descendant of one branch of the Blair family was to become one of the most celebrated of twentieth-century authors, even if he is better known as George Orwell than as Eric Blair.

In view of the arms which a later member of the family was to patent it seems our Blairs were descended from those who owned the estate of Balthaycock, a few miles to the east of Perth. In 1387 Patrick Blair of Balthaycock obtained the lands of Balgillo by a charter from King Robert II. Both Balthaycock, in the fertile plain of the Carse of Gowrie, and Balgillo, in Strathmore, are lands which the term 'blair' admirably describes. Another Blair was granted lands near Blairgowrie on which he built Ardblair Castle.

In 1627 Sir John Blair was one of the signatories to a curious agreement known as a 'Temperance Bond' by which parties agreed to take no drink other than within their own homes. Those who broke the contract were to be fined – 500 marks for the first offence and 100 marks for later ones – and participants were required to offer parts of their estates as some security on the contract. It seems that Sir John did in fact imbibe and thus was honour bound to pay James Haliburton of Pitcur several hundred marks. He reneged in paying so Haliburton seized the property in settlement of that somewhat paltry bond. The lands of Balgillo therefore passed out of Blair hands although they were long to remain claimants to its title. Try as one might one cannot really feel much sympathy for the Blairs. Surely if one is silly enough to enter into such a contract then one deserves to lose everything. One may, perhaps with some justification, conclude that to enter such an agreement one might have been already under the influence!

Another of the family, Peter Blair, supposedly lost everything in his support of the Stuart kings and so the family were compelled to move south. His youngest son, John, reputedly founded "John's Coffee House", a pioneering tavern made famous by Sir Walter Scott in his first novel *Waverley*. Scott tells us Blair was

> a gentleman of good family, who condescended, in order to gain a livlihood, to become the nominal keeper of a coffeehouse, one of the first of such places of the kind which had been opened in the Scottish metropolis. As usual, it was entirely managed by the careful and industrious Mrs B– – – –; while her husband amused himself with field sports, without troubling his head about the matter.

In our more egalitarian days we might wonder why it was not called 'Sarah's Coffee House' or 'Elizabeth's Coffee House' for after the death of his first wife he seems to have hastily married again, presumably because he needed an innkeeper as much as a wife!

John Blair also had two sons but they moved furth of Scotland to make their mark. The eldest, John, became a writer of some repute and gave his magnum opus and gave the delightful title *The Chronology and History of the World, from the Creation to the year of Christ 1753, illustrated in fifty-six tables*. One wonders why it was not fifty-seven or even sixty? He was for a time Chaplain to the Dowager-Princess of Wales as well as mathematics tutor to the Duke of York whom he accompanied on his 'Grand Tour' of the Continent.

Blair's younger son, William, was not only to become a Colonel in the Army of the Honourable East India Company but Governor of the old fortified town of Chunar, on the south bank of the Ganges. Col. Blair was to marry Jane Mackenzie, the daughter of Roderick Mackenzie, younger brother to the last of the old Earls of Cromarty who had seen their estates forfeited in the aftermath of the '45 Rising. The estates were later restored to direct descendants of the old Earl and when the title was revived in 1861 it was to Ann Hay Mackenzie, great-great-granddaughter of the last Earl and wife of the 3rd Duke of Sutherland.

Another of Peter Blair's sons, William, was a naval captain killed while in command of the 64-gun 'Anson' during Admiral Rodney's famous action off Dominica in the Caribbean in April 1782. Seven French ships were seized and their commander captured. The British had recently lost the American colonies and so this victory over the French was seen as a cause for national rejoicing. One of the lasting results of the celebration was the erection of an impressive cenotaph memorial in Westminster Abbey to commemorate the three captains who had lost their lives in the engagement. It is in effect possibly the earliest of British war memorials and it was erected at public expense by a grateful King and Parliament.

Thomas was the youngest son and he too served in India, rising to the rank of Colonel in the Army of the East India Company. He married his niece Jane, the daughter of Col. William Blair (Governor of Chunar) and Jane Mackenzie. On his return from India, Blair acquired thirty-three acres of land at Walton Grove – a sizeable plot if not exactly a vast country estate. The family had long lost their Scottish estates so now they were eager to secure English ones but, being proud of their Scottish roots, they had their own heraldic arms registered in 1815 – it was a variant of those of the Balthaycock Blairs. Colonel Blair also became heir to the claim on the Balgillo Estates but he seems to have as little success as his forebears in regaining them. He, therefore, had to be content with Walton Grove, although he did also have a London home in Welbeck Street.

By 1845, however, the Blairs had moved from Walton Grove. Henry Martin Blair, the Colonel's eldest son, had remained in India in the Honourable East India Company Service based at Madras. One of Col. Blair's daughters, Emily, had married Dr Richard Michell of Hertford College, Oxford in 1841. Henry Blair had married Caroline Brook and around 1860 he returned to England, took over the small estate at Farleigh Castle in Somerset and purchased Hyde Farm near Taunton. After his wife's death he settled in London in 1870 in a fine house in fashionable Stanhope Place, Hyde Park.

Their only son, Arthur Kindersley Blair, was to become an officer in the 71st Highland Light Infantry. Although modern writings have it that he attained the rank of captain there is no evidence for this. The *Army List* records have it that he became an ensign in January 1855. Although that commission was purchased (for the sum of £450) he was swiftly promoted. He became a lieutenant in June that year. His life in the army was to be as obscure as his earlier and almost all his later exploits but he did participate in the long siege and eventual fall of Sevastopol during the Crimean War. It is also likely that he helped garrison Malta before going to India where the 71st were active in quelling the Mutiny. Blair's may not have been a particularly distinguished or heroic piece of military service for he made no lasting impact on the 71st. After six years in the regiment he resigned supposedly to "live on his means" (*ILN*, 9 March 1889) and may, for a time, have assisted his father in his small estates in the West Country.

The historian of the HLI has informed us "the standard required for recruits for the 71st was a high one: height, five feet eight inches; chest thirty-four inches" (Oatts, 1952, 241). One assumes officers, like Blair, had also to be reasonably tall and well built. The Blairs had been long proud of their Scottish roots and no doubt derived great pride from seeing one of their number become an officer in a great Scottish regiment. Perhaps they were disappointed that he had not made more of it for they seem to have been a family who liked to aspire to greatness and hold on to tradition. Long after he had ceased to have any regimental link, Blair was referred to as being "of the 71st Highland Light Infantry". It is likely that, by 1872, he had taken up a post as an agent of the 3rd Duke of Sutherland but what is quite beyond doubt is that he had also found romance at home.

He had fallen in love with the youngest daughter of Richard and Emily Michell, Mary Caroline, and on 18 January 1872 the thirty-seven-year-old former officer and his twenty-four-year-old cousin were married in the delightful mediaeval church of St Peter-in-the-East in Oxford.

As the couple exchanged vows and smiled lovingly at each other they no doubt seemed in perfect and happy harmony. A year later their happiness was complete when their baby son, Arthur Guy Fraser Blair, was born. Sadly that happiness was to be of short duration for less than a year later the baby died. On 13 July 1876, however, their prayers were again answered when their baby daughter Irene Mary was born at Hertford College, Oxford.

By a strange quirk of fate therefore a rather nondescript ex-soldier from a rather pedestrian middle-class family had married his pretty young cousin. It was to be the first significant step in what was to prove a dramatic story.

PART TWO

Affairs of the Heart

True love's the gift which God has given
To man alone beneath the Heaven
SIR WALTER SCOTT – from *The Lay of the Last Minstrel*

CHAPTER SEVEN

A House Divided

Come as the winds come, when
Forests are rended,
Come as the waves come, when
Navies are stranded.
SIR WALTER SCOTT – from *Pibroch of Donuil Dhu*

Perhaps because his parents had been such spendthrifts, thanks to his mother's ability to build lavishly, the 3rd Duke of Sutherland turned his thoughts to ways which might make the estates more economically viable. Enterprising and enthusiastic, the Duke loved to enjoy himself and even when trying to make economic headway he coupled it with pleasure. All his policies allowed him to indulge in his love for machines and he delighted in the latest mechanical invention. He would derive the greatest of pleasure from seeing them in action and especially driving them himself - fire engines, steam ploughs and railway engines became his toys.

His love of innovation and technical progress led him in many directions. He was on board Brunel's *Great Eastern*, the massive iron-built steamship, during her trial when a dreadful accident occurred. Many of the sailors were badly burned and scalded when one of its boilers exploded and the Duke with great coolness and devotion gave every assistance to the wounded.

He learned like many before and since that one has to speculate in order to accumulate. He also discovered that it is easier to spend than to generate income. Like his father he tried to secure a sound infrastructure by building roads and bridges as well as harbours and slipways. He also endeavoured to ensure the local fishing fleets flourished.

Railways, however, was one of his great passions and especially their expansion in the Highlands. He was a Director of the Highland Railway and invested heavily in its development. He contributed largely to the line north from Ardgay across the Kyle of Sutherland to Golspie, while the section from Golspie to Helmsdale was very properly called "The Duke of Sutherland's Railway" for it was built entirely at his expense. For the line north to Wick and Thurso he was again the major contributor. It would be no mistake to claim that but for the Duke these lines would never have been built. He had his own station at Dunrobin and one of his chief pleasures was driving his very own railway engine. At the footplate of his engine, the 'Dunrobin', he was a familiar sight on the railway lines of the North. Not for nothing did he acquire the soubriquets "The Steam Duke' and "The Iron Duke".

Another great interest of his was in land reclamation, using steam ploughs – nicknamed "The Duke's Toothpicks" – to break up ground and clear stones and make the land capable of cultivation. These ploughs were "a sight to see and the whole enterprise attracted the attention of the whole country" (*Inverness Courier*, 23 September 1892). A friend recalled how he had

> set his hand to the task of reclaiming the wilderness of peat moss and stones . . . the legacy perhaps of the Deluge. Steam engines and steam ploughs, whatever money could buy and ingenuity could invent, were employed to do battle with the brute forces – the inertia – of rock and mud and submerged forests into which thousands of pounds sank year after year (*The Times*, 24 September 1892).

The scheme had been well intentioned but its location meant it would remain a pipedream – better situated land must ever be more economically viable. He spent something in the order of £250,000 trying to reclaim land near Lairg and in Kildonan. The lasting memorial of the enterprise was the granite obelisk he erected to commemorate his friend Kenneth Murray of Geanies who had been his chief advisor. Some land was cleared and a few farms marked out but, by and large, it was more earth shattering than deposit accumulating. The fact that the scheme failed however does not negate the high hopes and strenuous efforts.

It was believed he spent upwards of £500,000 on railways and land reclamation. The financial returns were minimal on the former and non-existent on the latter.

Making large amounts of money out of the Highlands has never been easy but for a spell, albeit briefly, it did look as if fortunes could be won. At Forsinard the Duke tried to gain oil from the peat bogs but it proved to be non-viable. In 1869 it looked as if prosperity had struck. Gold was discovered in Kildonan and this led to a 'gold rush'. Soon the Duke had organised 500 prospectors but apart from a few nuggets and some environmental damage there was not much to show when the last prospector left in January 1871. The false dawn had lifted and revealed the sad reality.

Gold being elusive the more mundane aspects of economic activity too were tried. In 1872 he revived mining operations at Brora coal mine and it was later stated there was "good reason to believe it will yield a good supply" (*The Times*, 12 September 1876) with a seam of coal 3' 6" thick. At Brora he also established locomotive engine works, a steam sawmill and brick and tile works where steam machinery was used to pulverise sandstone rock as well as work the clay supplies. It was hoped that it would all prove highly remunerative but sadly it came to little or nought. The coal mine sunk at Longton on the Trentham Estate proved a more successful venture. The flourishing industries and countless homes of the workforce of the Potteries required fuel – not much in Sutherland needed coal. Peat was available as a plentiful supply of fuel – there was no need to mine an alternative fossil fuel.

The Duke was much more successful on the social scene. He

and his wife entertained sumptuously. The Prince and Princess of Wales frequently visited them in Scotland and more regularly in England. The Shah of Persia stayed with the Duke at Trentham on his first visit to Britain and much admired his lifestyle. The Egyptian Khedive was a close friend who visited on occasion while Ferdinand de Lesseps, the builder of the Suez Canal, visited in 1870. Without doubt, however, no visit would have given the Duke greater pleasure than Garibaldi's.

The Duke was a sort of latter-day knight-errant always looking for adventure and chivalrous deeds to perform. Like his father and grandfather, he was supportive of social reform at home but he also much admired liberal national aspirations in Europe. This was not simply to be idle vociferous support. The Duke used his yacht to ferry patriots and supplies to aid Guiseppe Garibaldi and his Red Shirts of the Risorgimento in their attempts to secure independence and turn Italy into a political reality rather than simply a geographical expression. Garibaldi had become internationally renowned for his guerrilla tactics and his 'thousand heroes' had caught the imagination of almost everyone, even those who, like the Duke, tended to overlook their strongly republican ends.

When Garibaldi, who detested public acclaim, was persuaded against his better judgement to come to London in April 1864, the shy hero perhaps did not realise how rapturously he would be received. As soon as he landed he was met by the Duke of Sutherland and a welcoming committee and taken to London. The public response to the visit was overwhelming and so many clambering hands had clung to the side of the coach that when it reached Stafford House the coach simply fell apart, unable to take any more.

Inside the house Garibaldi was lavishly entertained at a reception in his honour. Few heads of state have been so fêted and during his ten-day stay at Stafford House there was a ceaseless round of balls and banquets, ceremonies and luncheons. It was overlooked that he was a man of the sword and not the cocktail stick and that he might have preferred something quite different. There were no idle moments and few opportunities to see the common people who idolised him. It is little wonder he wilted under the strain and took to bed much to the relief of the government. They had been unhappy to have him and the Queen disliked him. Getting him to return home was now easy. The Queen's physician advised rest and so he escaped back to Palermo and peace in the Duke's private yacht.

Garibaldi's visit had been akin to a boyhood dream come true. The Duke placed an impressive bust of that impressive head in the hall at Dunrobin. Garibaldi had been the Duke's hero and his undoubted charisma had endeared him to many. The Duke had been proud to know him and also proud of his own role in his hero's success. Few men get to meet their heroes: fewer still get to be part of their story. Garibaldi might have been of peasant stock and fought princes but a strong bond of friendship had been cemented between our Duke and his hero.

The Duke not only mixed amicably with princes and peers but seems to have quite been at home with lesser mortals. Lady Paget has written of "the Duke and his engineers, of whom there always was a strong sprinkling at Dunrobin" (Paget, 1923, 336). She has described a typical scene thus –

> At Dunrobin, besides the Indian princes, Turks and infidels, there were also what were commonly called "The Duke's engineers"...they were the builders, railway people and speculators. I once knew thirty–five of them come at one fell swoop and remain nearly a week . . . the Duchess implored me, with tears in her eyes, to remain and help her through this modern Egyptian plague. Then there was a certain smattering of adventurers and hangers–on . . . also a number of the Duke's staff and employees . . . I used to look down the long table and wonder what freak of taste possessed the Duke to collect this wonderful assemblage (Paget, 1923, 347).

To maintain his vast estates factors and sub-factors were needed and to make economic progress advisors and experts of all types were in demand. Men as well as machines would build the new Jerusalem. Probably among the company was the imposing figure of Arthur Kindersley Blair, for he has been described as 'agent' or factor to the Duke. As his name only figures in London directories it is perhaps safe to assume, if he was employed by the Duke, that he must have been based primarily at Stafford House. He might also have accompanied the Duke north for the season and latterly may have been assistant to the Dunrobin factor.

Blair's wife, some thirteen years his junior, turned many heads. She was contemporaneous with Cromartie, the Duke's eldest son, and he no doubt cast seductive glances at her but she clearly had a preference for the larger, more mature man. The rugged macho frame behind which lurked the boyish bravura of the Duke made her heart flutter. He too cast more than an admiring eye.

Duchess Anne, Countess of Cromartie had her own interests. On her estates she employed George Devey to prepare the master plan to turn the little spa resort of Strathpeffer into a town of some significance. Earlier, the great Scottish architect, David Bryce, had made some baronial additions to her family seat at Castle Leod.

Duchess Anne had been Mistress of the Robes to Queen Victoria from 1870 to 1874, some years after the death of Prince Albert but still during the period of Victoria's long withdrawal from public life. The demands of service to the Queen meant that much of life at home had to be sacrificed. She was unsparing in her attention. She was much loved by the Queen – but the Queen did not entertain this same high regard for the Duke.

The Queen had been concerned that the Duke of Sutherland might be a bad influence on her son, the Prince of Wales, but it may have been the reverse. The Prince had always been promiscuous and hardly required lessons from the Duke.

The Duke was one of "the Marlborough House set", a

group of rich, fun-loving aristocrats which the Prince of Wales gathered around him to share in his extravagant excesses. One of the more dangerous pleasures the Prince and Duke indulged in was fire-fighting. The Duke took a great interest in fires in the metropolis and had a fire engine of his own. He regularly attended fires in London and the 'amateur fireman' became a popular sight. His enthusiasm affected others and the Prince of Wales was a willing convert; Captain Shaw of the Chandos Street Brigade kept them informed of possible spectacular fires. It seems that "no matter what social engagement was in progress Duke and Prince . . . would race to Chandos Street, don firemen's uniform and climb aboard the next fire-engine" (Hough, 1992, 187). It was a high-risk venture and when the Alhambra Theatre was ablaze they were supposedly both at one point on the roof with hoses. Two firemen lost their lives as a result of injuries received during the blaze so that might have encouraged both Duke and Prince to seek safer pleasures elsewhere. The bedroom is less dangerous.

The Duke had somewhat uncouth ways and was renowned for his plain speaking. He was rumoured to have been considered for appointment as High Commissioner to the General Assembly of the Church of Scotland but instead he was passed over – perhaps he had been considered in the hopes that clergymen might encourage him to be a shade more moderate in language. He enjoyed smoking and was a key figure in the popularising of the smoking of cigarettes rather than cigars. The story is told that one day in the waiting room of Stafford Station he was having a smoke when a porter spotted him and told him that smoking was not permitted. The Duke promptly put out his cigarette but later lit up again. The same porter spotted him and was about to remonstrate when a passer-by pointed out to him that the smoker was none other than the Duke of Sutherland. The porter thus went forward and apologised. The Duke was suitably unrepentant but equally unimpressed by this sycophantic attitude. He carefully eyed the man before retorting "I took you for an honest man but I see you are a fool".

The friend of the Duke's recalled that a workman watching him set off on his train from Dunrobin and suitably clad for the role remarked to his mate "There, that's what I call a real duke – there he is driving his own engine, on his own railway, and burning his own blessed coals"(*The Times*, 24 September 1892). A more recent writer has it as 'bloody coals' (Stuart, 1982, 34). Most navvies are, perhaps a bit like the 3rd Duke, not renowned for their smooth talking and would more than likely have opted for the strongest term possible.

Although he enjoyed art and opera his principal interests were outdoor ones. He frequently took his yacht across the North Sea to fish for salmon off Norway. He was an expert horseman and a fine shot. Although he was Lord Lieutenant for Sutherland he mixed well and was popular with his tenantry. He was a generally kind and considerate landlord and when the Crofter's Commission visited the county they found that his sheep farms were let at comparatively low rents – in few cases did they have to make reductions and in some instances they actually raised the rents. If the Sutherlands had had a deservedly bad press in the past, George was keen to deal fairly with his people. It paid off, for he was much liked.

Big and bearded, the Duke dressed to please himself rather than others and although he cut a picturesque dash, Lady Paget, a frequent visitor to Dunrobin, "found the Duke a little unwashed and rough, but kind and *bon enfant*" (Paget, 1923, 297). She also recalled that

> The Duke's usual costume . . . was a red flannel shirt and a very ill–made Norfolk jacket of the Sutherland tartan over it, with a leather band, held together by an elastic ring. A knitted Glengarry covered his shaggy hair and his legs and feet were encased in the thickest of worsted stockings and the heaviest of hobnailed boots (Paget, 1923, 310)

Lady Paget did not consider him to be ultra-smart at dinner

time either. As far as she was concerned his attire was somewhat crudely provincial and she noted "in the evening he
swayed between blue serge and black velveteen, both made
by the Golspie tailors" (Paget, 1923, 310). In her perception
Golspie tailors did not quite produce the quality or finery of
their London counterparts.

He was especially fond of foreign travel – it was said that
there were "few ports of call in the civilised or uncivilised
world that were not familiar with him and his yacht (*ILN*, 1
October 1892). One of his earliest public trips was to Russia
for the Coronation of Tsar Alexander II in 1856 and while it
gave him a taste for travel it did not endear him to Russian
autocracy. He frequently cruised the Mediterranean. He was
one of the supporters of the Suez Canal scheme and visited it
during its construction in the company of William Howard
Russell of *The Times*, the pioneer war correspondent, and the
Prince and Princess of Wales. He returned again to be present
at its opening on 17 November 1869 and he had tried to form
a syndicate to take the canal over in 1871 when Egyptian
finances became shambolic. Though his attempt failed, he no
doubt applauded Disraeli's purchase, in 1875 and on behalf of
the government, of almost half the shares in the Suez Canal
Company.

He accompanied the Prince of Wales to India and although
there had been much criticism of the arrangements for the trip
and much debate over its financing, the visit proved to be a
magnificent success. On his return to Dunrobin he was given
a truly rapturous welcome. Crowds cheered, local Artillery
and Rifle companies paraded and 300 children carried
banners declaring "There's no place like home". A special
entertainment was laid on in the Exhibition Hall and a torch-
lit procession took place. A string of twenty bonfires carried
the celebration into the night. As a lasting memento the Duke
agreed to sit for a portrait to be hung in Dunrobin. He seems
to have been much liked.

When he arrived he was met by his children but his wife
stayed away. This may have been the first indication that all

was not well in the House of Sutherland.

But all was not well in the House of Saxe-Coburg-Gotha either.

There had been many affairs in the past but in 1877 the Prince of Wales had a 'love nest' built at Bournemouth for his mistress, the budding actress, Lillie Langtry. Even though it was somewhat unimaginatively named Red House because of its red brick walls below Mock Tudor upper storey, it was a charming house. There Bertie could visit Lillie and be as amorous as he wished and for a time they were happy. A stained glass window records their opinion that they did not care what others think. Lillie also etched their initials on one of the panes but the glass lasted longer than the romance. The house was later the home of Lillie's daughter (by Prince Louis Battenberg) and is now a most popular and comfortable hotel. After a spell as Manor Heath Hotel it is now more sensibly called Langtry Manor.

One of the Prince's "set" was the affluent banker, Cunliffe Brooks, who had not only enlarged Aboyne Castle on Deeside but had also acquired the estate of Glen Tanar where he entertained regularly and regally . On Lillie Lantry's first visit to Scotland she stayed at Glen Tanar House and has described her visit vividly. It rained continually and she lamented the fact that while "the men (were) eager for the massacre of the grouse and the stalking of the deer . . . there is nothing much for women to do" (Langtry, 1925, 114). She devised a sport which the other young ladies adopted enthusiastically – tobogganing down the stairs seated on Cunliffe Brooks' silver tea trays. Brooks was not amused and got his butler to lock away the precious items. Lillie, however, found the evenings to be happier for there was always dancing in the ballroom. She enjoyed the reels and scottisches and much admired the young gentlemen. She recalled that they "were handsome in their Highland garb, and a man has to be handsome to wear it!" Not everyone suited it quite so well as the young Gordons and she thought "mine host's rotund figure would have looked better more discreetly clad" (Langtry, 1925, 115).

Plate 4 Mary Caroline, Duchess of Sutherland
(at the time of her wedding to Sir Albert Rollit).

Plate 5 The Mausoleum at Trentham.
Last resting place of Mary Caroline, Dowager Duchess of Sutherland.

Plate 1 Dunrobin Castle from the gardens. The castle as it was at the end of the 19th century and as it would be known to Duchess Blair.

Plate 2 The impressive might of Carbisdale Castle.

Plate 3 George Granville William Leveson-Gower, the 3rd Duke of Sutherland.

She was as well to cast admiring glances elsewhere for her romance with the Prince was to come to an end. The Prince was to go on and have many affairs and a few mistresses. The Duke on the other hand seems to have found lasting contentment in the arms of one other woman.

Quite when romance first blossomed between the Duke and Mrs Mary Caroline Blair we cannot know. Lady Paget tells that on one of her visits he "spent half his life doing his accounts and the other half mooning by the sea with a lady who . . . had established a supremacy over him" (Paget, 1928, II, 297).

Lady Paget found Anne to be "not a happy wife or mother (who) looked for consolation to religion, which with her was a passion of her nature". The Duchess frequently read prayers she had composed to all the company gathered at the Castle. Lady Paget has delightfully recalled that –

> She (the Duchess) was in those days, the lowest of the low church, and one afternoon she took the whole party fourteen miles, in a cutting east wind, to Dornach (sic) where, after a copious tea at the inn, we went to Moody and Sankey's discourses at the Cathedral. I can myself always sympathise with any honest, earnest belief, and even if it enlists my enthusiasm, but the long drive back in the cold and dark so whetted the appetites of the company for the ten o'clock supper, at which champagne flowed very freely, that the conversation of some of the young men . . . did not exactly bear favourable testimony to the effectiveness of the sermon they had just heard (Paget, 1828, 298).

The Duchess became increasingly estranged from the Duke, and his endless visitors. She devoted her time more and more to praying, novel-reading and spending time with Lady Paget and a local clergyman, Mr Hewlett. We are told that "beyond the necessary civility, she took little notice" of the other guests (Paget, 1923, 329). Lady Paget tells

The Duchess's sanctum at Dunrobin was a delicious

sunny room, full of flowers and birds, high up in a corner of the old part of the castle. She had a huge couch, upon which she used to retire an hour or two before dinner, to read, and, when she was alone she used to remain lying down and had a tray brought in and ate her dinner whilst continuing to read her novel, for she was sentimental and liked love affairs (Paget, 1923, 330).

She did not, of course, find any pleasure in the Duke's love affair although she no doubt looked longingly and sentimentally to the 'good old days' when they both seemed to enjoy each other's company and shared so much. These days were now becoming a distant memory.

By 1878 things had become so bad that the Duchess purchased a fine villa at Torquay in order to escape from her problems. The elegant two-storey villa had been aptly named Bella Vista for it had magnificent views over Torbay but it was not a name she much cared for and so she changed it, to Sutherland Lodge before settling for the more imposing title of Sutherland Tower. It was not a tower but a handsome enough white-painted villa with ample accommodation and a little lodge house by the drive and all set within a one-acre garden with a fine collection of trees.

Their second son, Lord Tarbat, married Lillian, the daughter of another great clan chief, Lord Macdonald. Their eldest daughter, Lady Florence, married Henry Chaplin, MP for Mid-Lincolnshire and owner of Blankney Hall in Lincolnshire. Both events brought a little happiness. Sadly, however, following the birth of their third child in October 1881 Lady Florence died. A plethora of monuments in churches at Blankney, Golspie and Trentham testified to their love.

In February 1883 the Marquis of Stafford was thrown from his horse after hunting at Trentham. He was rushed to hospital at Newcastle-under-Lyme but was found to have only a dislocated shoulder. He was soon back at Trentham and the family rejoiced in his speedy recovery.

A few moments of happiness and a little shared grief and

anxiety brought the Duke and Duchess closer together for brief periods but true feelings and lasting love had disappeared into the North Sea haar. Their love had grown as cold as the marble monument in memory of Lady Florence.

Although he had been MP for Sutherland, George's interests were not national, political issues but local (Sutherland and Highland) or global (international) ones. He was not much interested in party politics at home but foreign affairs were an abiding interest. During the Russo-Turkish War he was one of the foremost supporters of the Turks and it is believed that he advanced considerable sums of money to the Turkish government when it was in the most grave of straits. Due to the dispute over the Turkish question he left the Liberal Party and henceforth supported Beaconsfield's Conservatives.

The Duke and Duchess may never have agreed politically for she was a diehard Tory while he was one of a long line of Whig grandees but by 1880 she was clearly unaware of her husband's growing respect for Disraeli and increasing disenchantment with the Liberals. She wrote to Disraeli, "I am anxious to tell you that I have, (as I once told you I would) let my tenantry know that I expect them to give their votes according to the principles always held in this house" (Hanham, 1978, 18). It was perhaps as much a gesture of defiance against the Duke as much as a declaration of independent action. It was certainly symptomatic of the fact that all was not well in the House of Sutherland. It was a house divided.

CHAPTER EIGHT

Death Can Be Fatal

He is gone on the mountain,
He is lost to the forest.
SIR WALTER SCOTT – from *The Lady of the Lake*

The name 'Dunrobin' means Robin's fort or castle and thus the early nineteenth century social commentator, Thomas Creevey, impressed by the fairy-tale nature of its picturesque spires and towers, referred to it as "Cock Robin" Castle.

Creevey had probably an eighteenth century nursery rhyme in mind when he coined his rather apt description.

> Who killed Cock Robin?
> I, said the sparrow,
> With my bow and arrow,
> I killed Cock Robin.
>
> Who saw him die?
> I, said the fly,
> With my little eye,
> I saw him die.
> (*Tommy Thumb's Pretty Song Book*, c. 1744)

It seems almost prophetic or at least ironic that in 1883 Arthur Kindersley Blair was killed, supposedly in an accident during a shooting expedition. Although many reports had the shooting taking place at Dunrobin, Blair was not shot there. He did however have close links with the castle for he has been variously labelled as 'factor' or 'agent' to the Duke of Sutherland at Dunrobin or simply as a 'dependent of the 3rd Duke of Sutherland'.

Let us therefore consider the shooting and as Sherlock Holmes would no doubt have remarked "the matter promises to be even more complex and mysterious than was originally supposed" (Doyle, 1890, 163).

It seems that no one shot Blair and no one saw the accident and yet if it was an accident a lot of people seem to have gone to a lot of trouble to conceal it. Normally when an accident happens people go to great lengths to show that it was accidental. On the other hand, if a crime is committed, the guilty party attempts to conceal the guilt by indulging in a cover–up.

The shooting of Blair seems to have been the subject of a massive cover-up. A great smoke-screen enveloped all those involved and has obscured the truth even to this day. Many people seem to have taken Holmes' stricture that "some facts should be suppressed" (Doyle, 1890, 112) very much to heart.

We may never get at the real facts but there are several distinct possibilities. Events prior to and subsequent to the shooting suggest that it was either a very convenient accident or it was indeed an act of foul play of the most grevious nature and successfully undetected.

On 10 October 1883 the intimation column of *The Times* carried the somewhat terse statement "On 4th October Arthur Kindernley Blair, the Highland Light Infantry, died aged 48, RIP". No information was given as to place or cause of death, no mention given of funeral arrangements and even his name was misprinted. The next day's edition had it correctly as Kindersley but no further details were added. It was surely a bald if not starkly mysterious announcement. It seems a sad, rather forsaken, end for an officer and a gentleman, a husband and a father. Certainly the very bare facts conceal his rather unbecoming end for Blair's body was found in a burn in Scotland. Whether by accident or design Blair seems to have left this world unloved even if at one time he had been respected and admired and no doubt loved. In the end he did not matter. In Scott's immortal words Blair seems to have been "unwept, unhonoured and unsung". His departure seems to have solved more problems than it created and yet even to this day we cannot be sure that it was accidental. It remains a problem. Suicide was considered a possibility at the time but equally one might suggest that it could well have been murder.

Let us therefore attempt to recount the whole story as far as is possible from this distance in time and space.

The Blair Family – Arthur, his wife Mary and little daughter Irene – spent frequent holidays at Bohespic Lodge, quaintly put at being "a mile and a bittock west from Tummell Bridge" in one of the most delightful parts of Perthshire. As its name suggests it was once the territory of the Bishops of Dunkeld, perhaps even the summer residence of the bishop himself.

Nearby are impressive falls and the Queen's View of Loch Tummel has a Royal seal of approval. Although it was not named after Queen Victoria but after some earlier monarch – Mary, Queen of Scots or Robert Bruce's wife, Isabella, being the two favourites – Victoria rather haughtily assumed it was so named in her honour. She noted in her diary – "at the end of the Loch, on a highish point called after me 'the Queen's View' though I had not been there in 1844". Victoria nonetheless on this occasion stopped to admire the view. She again noted in her diary – "we got out and took tea. But this was a long and unsuccessful business; the fire would not burn and the kettle would not boil". One can sense the exasperation when "at length Brown ran off to a cottage and returned after some little while with a can full of hot water, but it was no longer boiling when it arrived, and the tea was not good. Then it all had to be packed, and it made us very late". One can still grasp her impatience and irritation as one reads the words.

These were words written later in the day when she had had the opportunity to cool down – she was obviously much annoyed.

A few things are still there which Blair would have recognised. The little Free Church still stands but it is now a humble store at the Tummel Power Station and the commodious manse "embosomed in a grove of trees" has been re–christened 'White Lodge'. The little inn – Tigh na Drochait – where the Queen's coach horses were changed is now simply a row of private houses rather than a public house. The building overlooks the handsome Tummel Bridge, built by General Wade in 1730 and long known as Kynachan Bridge, thus possibly the general or his men frequented the old hostelry. The Tummel Valley Holiday Camp and the Bohespic Bar are the late twentieth–century near equivalents to cosy wee Tigh na Drochait.

A little to the west of the road which heads northwards to Trinafour and Calvine and which passes the Bohespics is the site of the house known as Bohespic Lodge – set a short distance back from the main road. Parts of its grey stone walls can be easily discerned, being about five feet or so in height. It has a lonely, sad look for it has been long neglected and abandoned. Densely-tufted tussocks of purple moor-grass now grow where once a family stayed and where our Blair family holidayed. Sheep seem to be the only regular visitors these days.

The official story is as follows: on the afternoon of 4 October Blair left the lodge to go shooting – it had not been a particularly good season for grouse and he may have been depressed about the lack of success. In any event as he trekked homeward in the late afternoon he slipped on the banks of a burn, possibly the one known as Allt Dalriach. At 5.30 pm his gun went off and the contents lodged in his body. He was barely 100 yards to the north-east of the farm at Dalriach and under half a mile from his home. His body lay with the discharged gun beside it. The noise of gunfire disturbed the evening quietness and people rushed to see the cause and rather surprisingly it was not someone from the farm but his wife who was first on the scene and found the body.

Suicide seems a rather unlikely cause of death for Blair could have committed it many miles from home and not within gunshot of farm or cottage. And then, why do it on a burnside at your doorstep when it could have been done indoors at home and at your own fireside?

If it was accidental then it must surely rate as among the most disastrously unlucky accidents of all time. Most guns that go off accidentally are wounding rather than fatal; bullets pierce limbs rather than lifelines; accidents hurt pride rather than terminate life. Blair's 'accident' was fatal. Dr Alex Crerar, the local doctor, came from his home at Ballinloan Cottage, near Kinloch Rannoch, in his pony and trap and though he was as early on the scene as possible he was too late to save Blair's life. Death, it seems, had been as sudden as it was surprising. Blair had died of a gunshot wound to his heart and left lung. It is perhaps little wonder that Dr Robert Irvine of Pitlochry, who was to examine the body in view of the suspicious circumstances, was wont to conclude that Blair had died of a "gunshot wound in breast" but added tersely "supposed accidental".

We do not know when, or indeed if, the local policeman was summoned or what form any investigation or enquiries took, if any did take place. Certainly the local constable seems to have lacked any of Sherlock Holmes' super-observant and mega-deductive qualities and instead seems to have accepted everything at face value. Although, even at that time some suspicion must have been aroused for a report must have gone to the Procurator Fiscal – the Scottish law officer who combines the role of coroner with that of public prosecutor – whose duty it is to initiate prosecutions and to investigate all suspicious, sudden and unexplained deaths and so eliminate the risk of undetected homicide. The fiscal sought the opinion of another 'expert' medical witness in order to assess the need for further investigation or prosecution and so Dr Irvine was asked to carry out the post–mortem.

It is worth noting that both ballistics and forensic medicine were in their comparative infancy in the 1880s and few doctors were well equipped to fully determine events. Dr Irvine simply speculated as to how Blair received his fatal wounds in his precognition or statement of facts to the Fiscal. The Fiscal in turn decided that no further action was neces-sary and yet information as to the place of burial and those who had carried out the interment was also added to the death certificate – presumably in case of the need for future exhumation and examination should further evidence come to light. Blair has, however, lain undisturbed, his body and his case forgotten. Indeed, Brent Council swept away the Blair tomb in Paddington Cemetery in a tidying up exercise in the 1980s so even time has not proved very loving to Blair or his memory.

At the time the incident attracted surprisingly little press coverage. The few newspapers that dealt with it passed it off as an "accident of a melancholy nature". A reporter for the *Perthshire Advertiser* carried out a piece of investigative journalism which was unique and is also a delight to read. It is worth quoting at some length.

The reporter had arrived at the Tummel Bridge Inn – "an excellent and well-conducted hotel" – where he met Miss Menzies, the hostess, and he has described the scene thus –

> I entered the hotel which, with its ornamental porch, &c, looks very neat and trim, and seems to invite the weary traveller to rest and refreshment. The landlady, a sonsy, respectable looking and middle-aged, unmarried woman, is a favourable type of a Scottish hostess. Polite and kindly, yet cautious and dignified, she makes her influence felt and respected by all she comes in contact with.
>
> "I hope you've had a good season in your hotel this year" said I, looking in the window of the bar-room which was open.
>
> "Well," replied she with a pleasant smile, "I cannot complain at all Sir; for we have been very busy indeed this year – more so than we have been for years past."
>
> "That shows," said I, "that you have been giving satisfaction to your customers when they come back and perhaps bring their friends along with them."
>
> She smiled again and said "I certainly try to do my best to please all that are so kind as to patronise my house."

"But," said I, "what a terrible accident that was that occurred in your neighbourhood the other day. Of course you can tell me all about it."

"Well," said she, in a cautious tone, "I don't know if I can tell you all about it, as perhaps I don't know the whole myself; but I am very sorry for Mr Blair. He was such a nice, frank gentleman, and everybody liked him. It was so sad how it happened to the poor unfortunate man."

"But how did it happen?" said I.

"Well," said she, "he went out that evening as the papers tell, with his gun; a shot was heard; and his body was found by his wife lying in the burn with the contents of the gun passed through his heart. Eh! what a cry there was through the place. The doctor was at once sent for; and he soon came; but what could he do? only tell what everyone knew well enough already, that the man was dead and could not be brought back to life."

"But," asked I, "how do you think it happened? was it an accident? or was it suicide?"

"According to the doctor," said she, "who is a very careful man, and weighs things on every side, it was an accident; and I suppose that's the most charitable view to take of the matter."

We do not need to be charitable – we wish to deal with the facts or even with the missing facts. Mr Holmes has advised us that "facts are better than theories" (Doyle, 1890, 142) but in the absence of facts theories will have to suffice. Is it worth noting that no words of sympathy for Mrs Blair are expressed in what is really a most charitable statement by Miss Menzies? If there was an investigation carried out by Perthshire Constabulary no records of the case now exist. Recent enquiries at the Procurator Fiscal's service and Sheriff Court also proved fruitless – if records were ever kept they have now gone. If the shooting ever provoked much investigation then it seems that then as now the records and the reports have been conveniently put to one side, misplaced or destroyed. And yet tongues obviously wagged, suspicions were aroused. Neither possible accident nor possible suicide seem to have satisfied the curious. There was no Fatal Accident Enquiry to put minds at rest. The *Perthshire Advertiser* reporter clearly had his doubts and headed his article with a string of Shakespearian quotations which suggest the mysterious rather than the mere accidental. Writing many years after the event, a *Northern Times* writer had this to say

> A mystery hangs over the death of Arthur Kindersley Blair . . . it may be that the facts might be made clear in reports filed at the period, but these papers are not easy of access, and, like most stories hushed up, sensational details have been circulated over the incident. Who fired the fatal shot was not legally proved, although suspicion pointed to a certain individual who would, for the good of the country, have been none the worse of a hanging.

If reports or files ever existed they seem to have long gone. Dead men, as they say, tell no tales. Those who hushed up the affair in 1883 have become as long forgotten as their actions.

If it was neither accident nor suicide then someone pulled the trigger. The question is who? The answer is never likely to be known and even if the underlying tenor of the above article seems to point the finger of suspicion at Mrs Blair, we can never know. She is without doubt the key suspect. She was there. She was having an affair with the Duke of Sutherland and poor Blair was in the way. Holmes' view that "women are never to be entirely trusted" (Doyle, 1890, 160) is not conclusive as to guilt of murder.

But what of the Duke himself? MacGregor has written that "the Duke was whispered to have been responsible" (MacGregor, 1965, 66). The possibility of getting rid of the husband of the woman you love may indeed have been "a stake for which a man might play a desperate game" (Doyle, 1902, 243).

With the death being at 5.30 in the evening the movements and activities of the Duke need to be examined. It is known that he was at Dunrobin on the Monday for he was able to be present at the gathering of the Rogart Educational Institute in the evening. He addressed the meeting and his wife presented the prizes. On Friday 5 October the Duke presided over the Review of the Sutherland Volunteers at Dunrobin after which he entertained them to lunch. Although there were two days shooting at Dunrobin the press reports are not specific as to whether the Duke was present or not. That being so there is a possibility that he could have been away from home between the Monday night and the Friday morning and could perhaps have been in or near Tummel Bridge. Were the 5.30 shots the fatal ones? Was Blair already dead at that time and with the Duke safely out of the way was it now possible to bring the shooting to light? Even with a killing at 5.30 pm it is surely possible to be back at Dunrobin the following morning. It seems that there is just enough time to get to and from Tummel Bridge. Indeed it seems likely that it was possible to get to and from this part of Perthshire in the times for which no cast-iron alibi exists.

But no one reported his being near the scene of the crime and no one reported him not being in Sutherland. Although he was living a very separate existence from Duchess Anne they nevertheless shared the same roof if not the same bed and no evidence suggests she thought him missing for any part of that week. Yet there are startling statements which run counter to all this – the *Glasgow Herald* was later to inform us that Blair was "accidentally shot by the Duke" (*Glasgow Herald*, 22 June 1889) and the *Evening Times* had it that "Mr Blair was killed by the Duke accidentally while they were out hunting" (*Evening Times*, 19 April 1893).

Mr Sherlock Holmes, during one of his investigations, was able to declare "I should like a few more facts before I get so far as a theory" (Doyle, 1915, 384) – we cannot allow ourselves that luxury. The deed is long done, the facts are few and it is unlikely that new ones will emerge. An absence of death–bed confessions has not got us any closer to the truth.

Doyle's hero has wisely informed us that one must "eliminate all other factors and the one which remains must be the truth" (Doyle, 1890,114) but it is difficult to eliminate any factors when information is so scant. Yet, while it is rather rash to conclude that Mrs Blair or the Duke shot her husband perhaps aided and abetted by the other and that it must remain "mere speculation" it is, as Holmes stated, "the only hypothesis which covers the facts" (Doyle, 1890, 150). Both had a motive; having a motive may not be conclusive as to guilt but it must surely be a necessary component of murder (as distinct from insane slaughter).

"The balance of probability" (Doyle, 1898, 115) seems to suggest murder although it was no doubt simplest to leave it as an accident. Dr Crerar obviously weighed up the possibilities and chose the trim solution. Others too readily fell into line – a later report simply stated that he "met his death from a gun accident which was due to his own carelessness" (*ILN*, 9 March 1889).

Sir Walter Scott has been referred to as "The Great Unknown" – the great unknown of this tale is the one who fired the fatal shot. It may well be that the suspicions of the time were correct and that either Mrs Blair or the Duke or both in collusion were responsible for Blair's death. The Duke was an acknowledged expert shot. It certainly holds the most appeal even if we cannot prove it beyond all reasonable doubt. If a crime was committed it truly was the perfect murder.

CHAPTER NINE

The Tangled Web

> *Widow'd wife, and married maid,*
> *Betrothed, betrayer and betray'd.*
> SIR WALTER SCOTT – from *The Betrothed*

A death near Pitlochry did not disrupt the social whirl of Dunrobin too much. A review of the Sutherland Volunteers had been held in the forenoon of 6 October but the dance scheduled for the evening "was postponed due to family bereavements and other circumstances" (*Scotsman*, 12 October 1883) and was held instead on 11 October. A party from Dunrobin then attended including the Duke and Duchess of Sutherland and their old friends, Ismael Pasha and his son, Ibrahim Pasha. Ismael may have been deposed as Khedive with his eldest son, Tewfik, now occupying his seat in the Viceregal palace in Cairo but they were old friends of the Duke's and were always welcomed warmly.

Within the House of Sutherland, however, things would never be quite the same again. One of the key stumbling blocks to the smooth passage of the love affair between the Duke and Mrs Blair had been removed whether by accident or design. Duchess Anne now felt even more threatened and insecure. She was well past her prime and her once renowned good looks had given way to an anxious worried countenance and depressive moods. While there may be some virtue in being the 'wronged' wife there is no happiness in it.

Happy marriages do not generally break down. Theirs had long been unhappy; it was difficult to pin-point when it had all started to go wrong. She tormented herself in reproach.

She prayed for reconciliation.

She had long looked forward to the day of her eldest son's wedding. She had almost given up on him for he seemed to be destined to remain single. Now he had found a quite delightful girl. She hoped they would be happy together.

Cromartie, Marquis of Stafford, at the age of thirty–three married Millicent, daughter of the Earl of Rosslyn, in St Paul's Church, Knightsbridge, on 20 October 1884. It was the wedding of the year and it was her seventeenth birthday and he had proposed to her when she was but a girl of fifteen. The bride looked magnificent in her pearl white satin gown, richly embroidered and trimmed with pearls and silver. The service was to be fully choral with nine bridesmaids in attendance, in cherry–red caps and carrying bunches of Parma violets, and three clergymen officiating. Among the near countless dukes and duchesses, earls and countesses and assorted other aristocrats of the congregation were the unmistakable figure of the Prince of Wales together with Princess Alexandra and Princess Christian. It was an impressive assemblage. So also were the wedding presents – it was said they "would have stocked Aladdin's cave" (Stuart, 1982, 36). Certainly the list of presents managed to fill two columns of *The Times* and included a gift from the Queen. Wedding celebrations did not confine themselves to London. At Lord Rosslyn's Fife estate tenantry dined at Dysart House. A great bonfire burned on the top of Ben Bhraggie as Golspie rejoiced.

It is probably in the nature of weddings to provoke gossip, much of it excited chatter rather than malicious tittle-tattle. The Sutherland-Leveson-Gower/St Clair-Erskine one was doubtless no exception. Millicent always referred to her husband as 'Strathy' (Viscount Strathnaver being his Scottish title) and Lady Paget tells that at the wedding "Milly stood a head higher than Strathy, clad in a grey shooting jacket" (Paget,1923, 376). It was perhaps an innocuous comment on Cromartie's diminutive stature but it may reflect more pointedly the differences between husband and wife. Perhaps, she was alluding to the possibility that the differences were not merely physical for they seem to have had little in common. Lady Paget may have wondered a little quite what the attraction had been. Looks and youth on the one hand: much wealth and a little maturity on the other? Would there be chemistry enough for a happy union?

Quite why he did not marry earlier or even someone of his own age group provides room for much speculation. We do not know the answer but one might surmise on the possible reasons. Had it been because of his own emotional immaturity? Had he been previously unlucky in love? Had he once found and lost someone or had he once been spurned? If the latter, by who? Had Mrs Blair done the spurning? Certainly Cromartie developed a very great, almost unnatural detestation towards his father's mistress. An ever widening gulf developed between father and son. Had they been rivals in love? Had this deep-seated resentment arisen because of jealousy?

A clue to Cromartie's personality can be found in a statement made to his young wife: "Remember dear, I do not like being interfered with or contradicted. I am so much older than you and cannot possibly change" (Stuart, 1982, 39). Cromartie did indeed like to get things his way. Compromise for Cromartie was impossible. He was ever the spoiled child and seemed incapable of communicating beyond the tantrum. His was a selfish, shallow, superficial world of show and glitter. He seemed incapable of true affection, probably because he had never had true affection shown to him.

In August 1885 Millicent gave birth to a little girl patriotically christened Victoria. The Queen had, in fact, given a shawl as a wedding present. It had been a difficult birth and Millicent had been much depressed for many months. A holiday seemed to be the solution. Cromartie therefore took her on a fourteen-month round the world cruise and when they returned in December 1887 they found little Victoria gravely ill. The child died in late January 1888.

Some growing up clearly had to be done. If Cromartie was incapable of that then Millicent must. On 29 August 1888 a son was born. He was to be George Granville and would one day be the 5th Duke of Sutherland. But also on that day a new, more responsible wife and mother had been born. Millicent was henceforth to prove herself a loving, caring individual. Cromartie, on the other hand, gained a son and heir and that was the result as much of duty as an act of love.

Duchess Anne had remained the Widow of Windsor's confidante and companion during four long troubled years and one can well imagine that it would have been an unenviable, demanding and difficult role, one that would have taken its toll of sanity and health in even the most robust of constitutions. Service to the Queen had exacted a heavy penalty and Anne was increasingly despondent.

At the time of Duchess Anne's son's wedding Lady Paget noted in her diary, "It's all been quite wretched for her" (Paget, 1923, 376) but regrettably we are not given the reason behind or the extent of her wretchedness. We can only assume that it had something to do with Mrs Blair or perhaps with gossip about the shooting of poor Blair.

Anne had cause to worry for her husband was now more deeply engrossed in his love affair with Widow Blair. The Duke and Duchess appeared happily together as proud and loving parents at Cromartie's wedding but it had been more show than substance for what had once been a rather discreet romance had now become the most open of secrets. Duchess Anne now no longer went to Trentham for Mary Caroline had more or less taken up residence there.

To make matters worse, Mrs Blair sold her family home in Hyde Park Gate and bought herself a fine town house at No 9 Park Place, St James', just a few yards away from Stafford House – in fact, it could not have been nearer or more threatening. Nowhere seemed safe from the presence of that woman!

Anne spent increasingly more time at Torquay. The people of Golspie were told that she had

> a bronchial affection which obliged her to leave
> Sutherland as early each season as her engagements

would permit and repair to her residence at Torquay,
the climate of which she had found to agree with her
(*Scotsman*, 27 November 1888).

It was, in a sense, only a little white lie – away from the
worry of watching her husband and his mistress she was
bound to feel a little better even if no less insecure. Princess
Alexandra visited the Duchess at Torquay and would no
doubt sympathise for she too knew the pain of seeing one's
husband take off with other women.

By 1884 Anne already seemed old for her years and lived as
a semi-recluse in two rooms in Stafford House. Her daughter-
in-law recalled "she spent much time lying on a sofa under a
red silk eiderdown. She surrounded herself with mina birds
and parrots, which perched all over the room and on the head
of the old retriever". Her grandson has written that she
"dined every day on chicken served by an old retainer whom
she bedecked with a blue ribbon as a kind of personal decora-
tion, and she insisted on eating alone" (Sutherland,1957, 38).

Anne regularly attended Crown Court Church – the Church
of Scotland's outpost in London – where she had her own
straight-backed narrow pew which was distinguished from
all the others by its highly-polished book board. There on
Communion Sundays she would sit with her personal piper,
clad in full Highland dress, by her side.

The Duke's trips abroad became longer and more frequent.
There was a long sail in the winter of 1886. Mrs Florence
Caddy in her delightful book *To Siam and Malaya in the Duke of
Sutherland's Yacht 'Sans Peur'* has captured some of the glam-
our and delights of one of these cruises to sunshine and spec-
tacle.

At the beginning of November 1887 the Duke and Mrs Blair
planned to set off for another winter cruise aboard the 'Sans
Peur' but instead the Duke had to take to his bed at Trentham.
The inflammation of the lungs caused such anxiety that even
telegrams wired to Stafford House bearing the terse message
"Duke not worse" were seen as good news. His condition
improved and by early December he was fit enough to leave

Trentham and join his yacht on the Mediterranean where he planned to spend some time recuperating. Anne was left alone and lonely.

She considered divorce proceedings but whether for the sake of the family or because her own health and even that of the Duke had posed problems enough she did not take any positive action. Perhaps she simply hoped that someday things might improve. Life became increasingly negative. The birth of grandchildren brought a few bright moments to an otherwise dreary existence but the long hoped for improvement proved elusive.

Things never did get any better – instead they only became more and more unbearable. The Duke returned and spent even more time with Mary Caroline and the Duchess rarely saw him. In the past there had been a pretence and public show of being together but even that sham ceased. They were now leading entirely separate lives and seldom under the same roof.

Lady Paget has recalled an incident which revealed the increasingly melancholy mood of the Duchess for whom life had lost all purpose. Lady Paget has written

> I had refused to go to Dunrobin since the Duke invited Mrs B– there, so the Duchess used to come up from Torquay to see me in London and the last time we parted she gave me a ring with two heart shaped pearls, bound together with diamonds, and asked me always to wear it in her memory (Paget, 1923, 464).

On 14 November 1888 the Duke set sail for the USA accompanied as ever of late by Mrs Blair. A sad Duchess arrived in London to bid him farewell. Rumour had it that she had hoped to go with her husband to America but that some of his guests as far as she was concerned could "not be regarded as congenial companions" and thus "saw fit to change her mind about going abroad" (*Northern Times*, 4 July 1935). Was it simply Mrs Blair she objected to? Had she perhaps given the Duke a sort of ultimatum and had Mrs Blair's presence there merely confirmed that he had made his choice?

She had hoped for so long that they could be reconciled and she had stuck by him in his illness but now painfully she realised that she had no future with the Duke. Did she then decide that without the Duke she had no future? Always a bit of a hypochondriac she now took to her bed and there illness took its fatal grip.

Within days she had deteriorated and died "of a sudden and mysterious illness" (*Northern Times*, 4 July 1935). It was reported that though she had been in bad health for some time "the acute symptoms to which she finally succumbed had not been in existence until ten to twelve days ago" (*Glasgow Herald*, 27 November 1888).

Had she taken her own life? According to Alasdair Alpin MacGregor "rumour had it that, broken-hearted, she had taken poison" (MacGregor, 1965, 66). Was it suicide or had she simply died of a broken-heart?

She had always been a kindly soul and it would certainly have been typical of her character had she expressed, as she has been reputed to have done, to her eldest son Lord Stafford, who had been with her at the end, that she knew the Duke and Mrs Blair would be married and "hoped all would be peaceful and happy" after that (Sutherland, 1892, 6). She had not known peace or happiness for many a long day. Now she was at peace.

One fellow attender at Crown Court Church was later to recall that "he noted among the crowded pews the face of a beautiful woman, whose agitated emotion made the tears trickle down her face leaving . . . curious channels down her cheeks" (Balfour, 1930, 176-7). That had been his impression of the Duchess. She had clearly been long unhappy. Lady Paget reckoned "she had never been a happy wife or mother" and that "her misery had been very great and she bore it with patience and firmness" (Paget, 1923, 464).

The Queen and the Royal Princesses called at Stafford House with wreaths to pay their last respects. Empress Frederick had burst into tears while the others had been greatly distressed. They had lost a loyal friend and had been much saddened by the Duke's treatment of her during her lifetime. They were more than saddened by his treatment of her in death.

We are told that the Admiralty were able to make contact with some fast naval vessels which in turn communicated with 'Sans Peur' but, rather than return, the yacht proceeded on its way. Rumour had it that when asked what should be done with the body the Duke simply retorted "Bury it". It seems a very likely response for the Duke had never been one to mince words. The Duke may have been many things, but a hypocrite he was not.

The press reported more generously that when the Duke received news of his wife's death "it was impossible for him to return in time for the funeral and he has continued his journey (*Moray & Nairnshire Express*, 1 December 1888). The Queen had not been amused!

At Stafford House the body, in its splendid oak coffin and covered with crosses and floral wreaths, lay for a time at the foot of the grand staircase. Where she had once been a vivacious society hostess she now lay a pathetically tragic figure. Eventually the great glass doors opened and with heavy rain and leaden sky the Countess of Cromartie left Stafford House for ever.

She was not taken to the Sutherland Mausoleum at Trentham but instead was taken to her beloved Torquay where she was laid to rest in the cemetery. Although neither the Queen nor Prince of Wales attended they were represented by the Earl of Limerick, Lord in Waiting to the Queen and Major-General Ellis. Henry Wright, the Duke's private secretary, represented his master. Romance had long gone – now there was no whiff of pretence. Even loyalty was not rewarded – those whom she served and loved in life had merely sent deputies in her death.

A stained-glass window was later placed to her memory in the magnificent church at Babbacombe. In Strathpeffer a new church for which she had earlier given the site was dedicated to her memory – it was called appropriately enough St Anne's and designed by the able architect of Highland churches, John Robertson.

In Golspie, as a mark of respect, on the day of the funeral all the shops and other businesses, as well as the school, closed for the hour between noon and one o'clock. The flags flew at half mast from the towers of Dunrobin.

PART THREE

Sunshine And Shadows

Twist ye, twine ye! even so
Mingle shades of joy and woe,
Hope and fear, and peace and strife,
In the thread of human life
SIR WALTER SCOTT – from *Guy Mannering*

CHAPTER TEN

A Romantic Interlude – Florida Cocktail

The orange flower perfumes the bower,
The breeze is on the sea.
SIR WALTER SCOTT – from *Quentin Durward.*

There had been pioneering work under previous bishops but with the consecration of Edwin Gardner Weed as Bishop of Florida in 1888 a new and greater emphasis was placed on this missionary role. In his Episcopal Address Weed declared "our Diocese is pre-eminently a missionary diocese . . . The Church is constantly finding her way into new fields, and making new advances into the 'terra incognita', of the southern portion of the state" (Cushman, 1965, 177–8).

People from the increasingly densely populated and industrialised cities of the north desired to escape to the sun and tranquillity of the south. New waves of immigrants, many of British stock, were also eager to make new homes and new lives for themselves in the warm, hospitable climate of Florida. The opportunity for the Episcopal Church to expand therefore constantly presented itself. During the winter of 1886–87 Rev. Gilbert Hall White of London visited relatives and friends in Pinellas county and he was one of several English clergymen who briefly served British settlers. A more permanent church presence seemed to be demanded.

But it was not only the churches which saw the opportunities, indeed the church was simply following in the wake of others – those with more temporal thoughts first saw the

99

potential. Hamilton Disston was an entrepreneur with a range of interests from sawmilling to land speculating – presumably Disston in Oregon owes something to the man – and he purchased many thousands of acres of Florida from the US government. The now thriving little city of Tarpon Springs owes much to Disston and his family home can still be seen on Spring Avenue.

Another of those who saw the possibilities in Florida was Anson P. K. Safford. He had made a fortune in the silver strike in Arizona and had become the first Governor of that territory and the city of Safford is named in his honour. In 1882 Safford retired and seems to have invested much of his fortune in purchasing land from either Disston or the government. He thus set up his home in Florida and in the small township that was developed into Tarpon Springs.

Florida had become a Spanish possession in the sixteenth century and although it had briefly been taken by the British in 1763 with General Grant of Ballindalloch as Governor it was basically to remain a Spanish colony until purchased by the USA in 1819. By the latter decades of the nineteenth century the Pinellas region of Florida in particular was beginning to establish itself as the world's premier citrus culture region while Tarpon Springs and its environs was to develop as one of the most exclusive winter resort areas of Florida's west coast.

Disston and Safford, having invested heavily in land purchase, now sought rewards and thus promoted the area by advertising widely and drawing attention to its mild healthy climate as well as its scenic splendour. They began to subdivide their land holdings and sell off smaller parcels and thereby make an even greater fortune for themselves.

To set the seal of approval on the area a big name was needed and there were few more exclusive pedigrees than that of George Granville William Sutherland-Leveson-Gower aka the Duke of Sutherland. Safford was honoured that his "first big sale" was a parcel of 40 acres of land at the north end of Lake Butler (now Lake Tarpon) which he sold to the

Duke of Sutherland. 'The Duke' (or more precisely 'The Dook') as he was to become affectionately known by the locals then proceeded to have erected a two-storey cypress-built "small but comfortable house" (*Glasgow Herald*, 1 March 1889). Sutherland Manor, a typical southern building with shingle roof and walls of timber weatherboarding and long porches or verandahs, was also set on a superb hill-top location. While not exactly of palatial proportions, we are told, it was commodious enough with spacious living-room, dining-room and sitting-room downstairs and two high-ceilinged bedrooms upstairs. Large fireplaces provided the welcoming fires for the public rooms as well as heating the principal bedrooms. The kitchen was sensibly located in a detached annexe as were the servants' quarters.

Its walls of white plaster gave it a clean and fresh look and were no doubt the perfect foil for the treasures on display, for the home was both extravagantly and tastefully furnished. Old money has a style and a grandeur that the new can rarely emulate. Not only was the Duke accustomed to grand surroundings but he, or at least his companion, would be eager to impress the 'nouveau riche' of Florida.

While it was reported that the Duke was "living quietly . . . devoting most of his time to hunting, shooting and fishing" (*Glasgow Herald*, 1 March 1889) it was certainly not a life of lonely sad widowerdom. It was to this house that the Duke brought Mrs Blair and there she "shared in his sports and pastimes" and perhaps even, in Sir Walter Scott's delightful phrase, indulged in "the ancient and now forgotten pastime of high jinks". They could also enjoy afternoon tea out of doors quietly together or with a few friends. At other times they entertained lavishly and Sutherland Manor was to become the principal "social centre" for the élite of the area with "elaborate parties". The Duke's motor yacht 'Sans Peur' was used to give excursions through the exotic bayous of the Anclote River. A cycle path was formed to link the estate with Tarpon Springs itself and was no doubt much used by Mrs Blair's young daughter.

The Duke was regarded as something of a social lion – his name supposedly headed the guest list of the Peninsula Hotel, at Tavares, while he was regarded as *the* attraction at every social function for miles around. Locals were delighted to have him in their midst and the little town of Palm Harbour briefly changed its name to Sutherland, presumably in his honour. A lake near Dunedin also acquired the name of Sutherland.

Tarpon Springs was rapidly developing. Not only did retired businessmen from the north make it their home but also wealthy individuals from the cities who desired holiday homes. Handsome and substantial winter homes were built for these incomers. They came for many reasons but chiefly to enjoy the sunshine and the medicinal spring waters and to partake in a host of recreations such as sailing, swimming, fishing and picnicking. They also came for fun – for a season of lively yet decorous entertaining and the Sutherland household was part of this elegant and lively set.

Although Mary Caroline Blair was regarded as "something of an enigma to the neighbours" (*Glasgow Herald*, 1 March 1889) the problem was solved when it was announced, in mid-February 1889, that the couple had become engaged. Rumour soon spread that a licence for marriage had been issued and that she would soon become the new Duchess of Sutherland. Although gossip had it that they were to be married in Pensacola (between Tallahassee and New Orleans) later that month it was either an uninspired guess or a deliberate red–herring, even if "semi-officially announced" (*Moray and Nairn Express*, 16 February 1889), for they had no doubt, by that time, firmly settled on having a church wedding in the little town of Dunedin, some ten miles or so to the south. The very name 'Dunedin' had an affinity with the Duke's own Scottish home 'Dunrobin'.

Dunedin had originally been named Jonesboro in honour of George L. Jones, its first County Commissioner, who had opened a shop there in 1870 but the arrival of two Scots who opened a rival store resulted in a petition to the government for the official postal designation to be Dunedin and it was that name that stuck. Thus the little town of Dunedin (which they named after Edinburgh, the Scottish capital) was born and to this day the town has cherished its Scottish links and retained a Scottish flavour. It has Highland Games; Dunedin High School has a pipe band and a kilted piper adorns their publicity leaflet which also tells us that Dunedin's bands "have won many competitions with their Scottish music and dancers". The town is now also twinned with the Scottish town of Stirling.

A few months after his consecration as Bishop of Florida Weed conducted a service in Dunedin. Although it was yet without a church the need for one was self-evident and Weed considered appointing a missionary for that corner of Florida. The local people too had decided that they ought to have a church and under the inspired leadership of Mrs Jones (a sister of the Bishop of New Orleans) and Mrs William Simpson began to set about getting one for themselves. They obtained a site from Mr Simpson and got the timber to build it from Simpson's yard and then hired Mr Osborne, the local carpenter, to construct it.

The Rev. William Noyle had been seconded from England and after a spell as Rector at St Thomas's Church in Eustis he became the missionary for the Dunedin area and thereby vicar to the small but growing band in Dunedin. He was soon to become the Archdeacon for the Gulf Coast.

The Duke seems to have donated handsomely towards construction costs even if he did not do any manual work. Archdeacon Noyle on the other hand rolled up his sleeves and put his old carpentry skills to use in speeding on its construction and creating its furnishings. Both men had a vested interest in its early completion.

The Church of the Good Shepherd was an elegant if humble neo-Gothic church built almost entirely of timber. Small lancet windows let the sunlight stream into its sanctuary while its door was reached by mounting a flight of some four steps at the cute little porch at the side of the building. The porch provided a welcome feature of interest on what was a simple if not rather austere building – the porch would obviously become the ideal spot for posing for photographs for the wedding albums. Its steeply-pitched timber roof was terminated by a tall cross while a separate structure of no great beauty and of latticed timber formed the bell tower. The bell would summon the small congregation to worship and the homely sturdy simplicity of the church no doubt endeared it to everyone.

4 March 1889 was an important day in the history of the United States. It was the very day when Benjamin Harrison was inaugurated as the 23rd President of the United States and in his honour Harrison Avenue connects the towns of Dunedin and Tarpon Springs.

Dunedin had its own very special reason to rejoice on 4 March for not only did the completed church open its doors for the very first time but its first vicar, Rev. William Noyle and Miss Amy Thomson were married – and obviously at the first wedding to take place in the little church.

The siting of the church itself almost ensured it would be buried in the bloom of the orange orchard but internally it was profusely decorated in blossom and foliage for the villagers were proud of their achievements and delighted in the happiness of their pastor. They had crowded into the church for that ceremony but it was simply the prelude to *the* main event.

Exactly one hour later the church was thrust into the international limelight when Bishop Weed again officiated although this time he was assisted by Archdeacon Noyle at the second wedding – the marriage of the Duke of Sutherland to Mrs Mary Caroline Blair. The historian of the Episcopal Church in Florida has been rather coy for he has written that Mrs Blair was simply "an English resident of the area" (Cushman, 1965, 179) whereas we know she was in fact resident with the Duke and that they had long had a close and intimate relationship.

Oranges and lemons,
Say the bells of St Clement's.

The words of the old nursery rhyme have an appropriate peal for they bridge the miles between the sunshine and citrus of Florida and the grey city churches of London. Past actions and present animosities had made a wedding at Dunedin seem a bright spot on what might be a dark future. It had been decided to have a quiet wedding with neither honeymoon nor wedding tour but the original intention of having a quiet lunch at the Duke's home had given way to a meal with friends. This was a day to be celebrated and enjoyed.

Rumours had persisted for some time about the impending match and when the news broke that a marriage licence had been obtained Dunedin was agog in excitement for it was the only likely spot and within easy reach of the Duke's residence. Now the big day had dawned.

Mrs Blair and her daughter were driven to the church from the village inn in the only available carriage. The Duke and the rest of the company walked to church.

At 11 o'clock the bridal party entered with Mrs Blair carrying a huge bunch of roses and resting on the arm of Mr John Knight, an old friend and well known yachtsman and adventurer, together with the maid of honour, the bride's twelve year-old daughter, little Irene Blair, and two other bridesmaids, Miss North and Miss Smith. On their entry Bishop Weed and the Archdeacon stepped out of the vestry and were soon followed by the frock–coated Duke. They were scarcely at the altar when Mr Knight and the bride arrived. The simple ceremony was soon over and the smiling newly-weds stepped out into the sunshine.

This second wedding had caught the imagination of everyone and they all crowded around in excitement. The ladies looked in delight at the Duchess's dress of white silk trimmed with coffee–coloured Chantilly lace while her white bonnet was trimmed with ostrich plumes and velvet and decked out with gorgeous diamond pins. Miss Blair's dress was of white nun's veiling trimmed with lace and she had a broad white sash as well as a white hat decorated by mauve plumes. Miss Smith was dressed in white silk elaborately embroidered with roses and she also wore a great diamond horseshoe which the bride had given her. Miss North wore a costume of grey cloth with matching bonnet.

Although County Commissioner Jones lost out in the naming of the place his wife obviously did not bear many grudges or if she did this was not the day to show them. At her small hotel she was the hostess for the small party of about a dozen as they joined together at midday for the wedding breakfast. Bishop Weed proposed the toast to the health and happiness of the bride and groom. In his reply the Duke thanked all the people of Florida and expressed his best wishes for their future and hinted strongly that not only had he found his greatest happiness there but that he would like to make his permanent home in their midst.

It was not to be so – storm clouds were already gathering beyond the horizon and grey clouds would soon mar the vast sea of blue.

CHAPTER ELEVEN

Trouble and Strife – 'Duchess Blair'

Touch not the cat (without) a glove.
SIR WALTER SCOTT – from *The Fair Maid of Perth*

It had been a glorious day in every sense yet there was a dark cloud on the horizon. All that marred the great day was the fact that the Duke's family had not taken kindly to the idea of the wedding. When he had written to tell them of the proposals these had been very coolly received and thus the love-sick pair were resolved to marry sooner rather than later.

Rumour had also reached England that the Duke had begun negotiations with Mr Vanderbilt, the American millionaire, regarding the leasing of London's Stafford House which the Duke found increasingly costly to maintain. This was another issue which ensured that when they did return to England at the end of April, old animosities would be to the fore and would have gained fresh fuel.

Perhaps fearing that Stafford House might be sold from under them, the family had not been idle. When the Duke and Duchess returned they found the private rooms had been stripped of all ornaments and they were informed that his daughter, Lady Alix, had placed numerous packing cases of objects in a warehouse. Only papers in the Duke's private room remained, everything else had been taken. A letter was hastily dispatched to Lady Alix who promised to return all the papers when she had unpacked. It did not seem to bode well for the future.

About a week later the Duke and Duchess visited Torquay to find out what had become of Sutherland Tower. The Duke offered it to the Duchess as her holiday home but she did not much care for it so declined the offer. A few objects were selected which the Duke especially valued but most of the contents were left intact. The Duke hoped that Lady Alix might perhaps accept the house but it was not to be and thus the property was sold.

It was not simply the Duke's children who frowned on his new wife. Lady Paget tells that his brother, Lord Ronald Gower, was "staying away from England to avoid the Duke whom he will not see after his marriage" (Paget, 1923, 498). Where once the Duke had been a leading social figure and popular with the Royal Family, he was now ignored and shunned by almost everyone.

During the summer some attempts at family reconciliation were made. The fine old Uppat House near Dunrobin was offered to the Marquis of Stafford but he instead opted for the lodge at Loch Choire, presumably because it would be much further away from his step-mother. Lady Alix remained hostile and would only arrange to see the Duke if she was forewarned that the Duchess would not be accompanying him. In September Lord Stafford spent a few days at Dunrobin and revealed his mother's hopes that when the Duke and Mrs Blair were married "all would be peaceful and happy". To which the Duke retorted, "You should have told us that before". Stafford added, by way of excuse, "Oh, that was meant for the family". The Duchess, never one to stand meekly aside or even to daintily test the water when she could brutally put her boot in, added her own helpful assessment – "Of course it was meant for the family; there was no doubt (that) your father and I should be peaceful and happy; she meant she hoped *all* of us would be so together" (Sutherland, 1892, 6). Lord Stafford retreated. The Duchess was later to tell her mother of the incident and the Duke mentioned it to his son-in-law but Stafford denied the conversation had ever taken place. There was to be no peace!

In the autumn the question of the need for a suitable English Dower House was discussed. Since Duchess Harriet's Cliveden and No. 2 Hamilton Place had been sold because Duchess Anne had expressed a wish to live in Torquay the choice of suitable properties in the present domain was not wide. In fact, only one property sprung readily to mind, or at least to the Duchess's mind – Tittensor Chase, near Trentham. It was a picturesque black and white neo–Elizabethan house of largely 1856 vintage. Though George Devey may have had a hand in it, it was very much a creation of the Trentham architect, Thomas Roberts. Although the Marquis was bitterly opposed to the idea the Duke decided to let the Duchess have a twenty-one year lease of Tittensor Chase.

In the spring of 1890 Lady Alix asked her father if she could have Little Hales, a house near Lilleshall, where her brother, Lord Stafford, was residing. All the furniture from Torquay was brought north and used to equip Little Hales for her. The Duke hoped, by agreeing to her every demand, that all his private papers might be returned. The papers were never to be returned and Lady Alix now maintained that her mother had destroyed everything prior to her death (a fact suggestive of suicide?).

In August the Duke took the Duchess for a tour round Sutherland. They stayed in the Duke's splendid lodge at Lochinver (now the Culag Hotel) and as the Duchess had recently sold her London house at No 9 Park Place, St James' to Lord Salisbury's eldest son, Viscount Cranbourne, for £10,000 it was jokingly discussed over dinner one evening that she might spend her "windfall" by building at Lochinver. The idea did not take root there, but at Tongue the matter was again discussed with more seriousness and she was more receptive to the idea. A site of five acres in front of the factor's home (the House of Tongue) was agreed and the Duke's solicitor was instructed to draw up the necessary documentation in order to feu the site. The Sutherlands were later to note that "plans for a shooting lodge were got out" thus implying that they were already in the plan chest and therefore presumably

designed by William Fowler, the Duke's Sutherland architect
(if not by Roberts or Devey), rather than by an outside architect. Work on the shooting lodge began in March or April
1891. It still stands as a handsome two-storey lodge with oriel
windows and tile hung walls. It is almost an English suburban villa set in the Highlands of Scotland.

The Staffords appear to have spread rumours that this was
to be the Dower House and press reportage fuelled the speculation. The Duke then considered disentailing a suitable site
and presenting it to the Duchess for a dower house should she
be left alone. This led to a long, costly and acrimonious battle
in court which was found in the Duke's favour. On appeal the
matter was upheld in the Duke's favour but the Marquis
resented it and threatened to take the matter to the Lords.

The death of Lady Alix at the early age of twenty-six did not
result in any respite in the family squabble. The Duchess, we
are told, entered a room in which Lord Stafford was
discussing things with his father and rather hurt she recorded
how Lord Stafford's "conduct to her was most rude". He, it
seems,

> neither rose from his chair, nor took the slightest notice
> of her; and the moment she said "I hope this sad death
> may be the means of making you feel more kindly
> towards us," he jumped up, said roughly that he had
> "come to discuss business with his father, and would
> not speak to her," and left the room. (Sutherland, 1892,
> 17).

It is hard to see who bore the greatest degrees of pique –
those who feel slighted or those who do the snubbing. Thus
war continued.

The Duke, however, did not restrict his squabbles to the
family. In August 1891 he took legal action against
Staffordshire men, over coal and mineral rights on land leased
to them, and in supposed breach of a deed of 1783. Neither
the Duke nor his agents had any knowledge of any rights
until a few years earlier when the deed was being referred to

for another purpose (presumably to find cause to sue some-one else at court!). Mr Justice Vaughan Williams, however, was unimpressed by the age, the chance discovery, or the words of the deed and stated that "there are well-known apt words which could have been used and which would have put the matter beyond controversy but they were not used and yet the deed is skillfully and artificially drawn by the conveyancer" (*The Times*, 4 August 1891). The defendants were to win the case; the Duke had to pay costs. The Duke was unhappy with this outcome and appealed against the decision but in January 1892 the Judges, having considered the matter, felt that the original verdict was the correct one and that "the appeal must be dismissed with costs" (*Law Reports*, 1892, 486).

Although Lord Stafford had removed a substantial amount of trees at Lilleshall, he took umbrage at his father cutting down trees at Trentham, some believed to be of great age and beauty. He tried to get an injunction to halt the felling and the case came to court in March 1892. Mr Humbert, estate agent and surveyor, for the Marquis, stated that trees had been marked ready for felling. Mr Collins, the Duke's forester, on the other hand, maintained that the trees had been marked so that the Duke's attention could be drawn to them and that it was normal practice to identify trees for inspection in this way. The point that they might be inspected with a view to removal seems to have been overlooked. In any event Mr Justice North, in his usual slow deliberate way, noted that "a coolness existed" between   Stafford and his father. On Stafford's notion that the Duke was felling trees to be vindic-tive, Sir Ford North stated "there was no more reason for inferring that the Duke was acting vindictively than there was that the Marquis himself was acting vindictively in bringing the action" (*The Times*, 30 March 1892). It may not have been a flash of brilliance but it was typical of the sound rather matter-of-fact ways of Mr Justice North. He therefore ruled that the Duke was at liberty to fell trees and gave considerable praise for the Duke's management of his estates.

The Duke took much pride in his estates and although the general public had long had access to the policies at Trentham it was not a licence for mayhem. The Duke had, in fact, caught a woman digging up plants and had her prosecuted "in order to protect and preserve the grounds for the benefit of the public" (*Evening Times*, 27 September 1892).

In October 1891 the Duke suffered some serious illness while at Dunrobin and although the Duchess wrote to Stafford inviting him to the castle "a curt and ungracious answer" was the response (Sutherland, 1892, 21).

The Duke now had to pay hefty legal fees in the Disentail case and over the "Timber Case", both the result of his son's actions, so when he was presented with a bill for medical treatment for Lady Alix which should have been paid by Stafford, as executor, the Duke decided enough was quite enough and Stafford was given a reduced allowance. This only further aggravated the rift. Lord Stafford, maintaining that he could not now afford the upkeep of Lilleshall, moved out and when the Sutherlands took possession in the spring another squabble ensued over plate and furniture which Stafford had apparently removed.

It might never have been a very happy family. Now it was a decidedly unhappy one. The only people likely to have been content with the run of events had been the solicitors, doubtless neither slow nor low in their accounting.

In the early summer of 1892 the Duke and Duchess decided to set down on paper a record of the treatment meted out to them by their family. If they were ever eager to smooth things over one cannot but conclude that a paper setting down every trifling grievance seems the wrong way to achieve peace and harmony. In fairness, if the record of all the events which sought to explain "how they had been absolutely forced into the sad quarrel" is a true one then they did attempt to be accommodating, even if a bit self-righteous in the appraisal, while others were ever spoiling for a fight.

They do not seem to have considered that writing and printing such an account could only further fuel the quarrel. The

Duke was never known for his tact but in reading the document one senses the Duchess's hand behind the pen – it is tactless. Although it purports to be a joint exercise, unmistakably it is her work. She had no reason to be grateful to the Duke's children for their past treatment of her and she seemed to be getting all she wanted at their expense by continually pitting the Duke against them. A reconciliation might mean a reduction!

On 4 August, the battle at its fiercest and the Duke at his weakest, he had a fresh will drawn up. The Duchess, together with Walter Michell (her brother) and the Marquis of Dufferin and Ava (a family friend of long-standing and former Viceroy of India), were to be executors. The will was very much in the Duchess's favour. In the family battle she was becoming victorious.

In the late summer of 1892 the question of a suitable Scottish Dower House remained unresolved. After much discussion and after numerous visits the house of Cambusmore was selected. It is a sprawling Victorian lodge with a host of dormers and gables and whitewashed walls, and has a southerly exposure overlooking Loch Fleet, a large salt water basin a few miles south of Golspie. With large entrance hall, dining and drawing rooms tastefully decorated in white and fine panelled smoking room on the ground floor and with about ten bedrooms on the first floor it was a commodious and comfortable house, ideal for any Dowager. Its grounds consisted of lawns and shrubberies which sloped gently down to the road and railway line which ran along the lochside.

It was to get little further than the discussion stage.

The Inverness Northern Meeting was to be held on Saturday 24 September. They were looking forward to it with great excitement – the Duke had entered their names for the balls, organised a special train to be driven by his very own private engine and booked a suite of seven rooms in the comfortable Caledonian Hotel. It had been a hotel they had frequently used, being a mere two minutes from the railway station, and their windows had a splendid outlook over the river. Mr Alexander McFarlane knew how to care for his guests and he had recently refurbished and extended the hotel and proudly advertised the fact that it was "patronised by the Royal Family and most of the nobility of Europe".

Although the Duke had largely dropped out of the old social whirl they still enjoyed visiting picture exhibitions and other public functions but this meeting was one of their favourite events. They liked the company there and the Highland Gathering, Games and Tournament all added up to a hectic and enjoyable few days. The ball was the highlight with the music as supplied by Mr H. Dambmann's orchestra always appealing. Only an emergency would prevent the Duke and Duchess from going to Inverness.

On the Wednesday prior to the big day, however, the Duke took violently ill with, what was believed to be, a stomach upset and chill but it soon "assumed an alarming form". Dr Simpson of Golspie was called and after examination, he expressed his great fears. During the day the Duke's condition worsened. A telegram was sent summoning medical aid from Edinburgh. The Duke (or the Duchess) perhaps sensing death was fast approaching summoned the Duke's Golspie solicitor and a codicil was added to the will. It was brief – if the transference of Cambusmore to the Duchess was not through in time she was to receive an enhancement of £50,000.

One newspaper told its readers

> The end came sooner than was expected. Telegrams received at Inverness last night represented the Duke's illness as giving cause for anxiety, but the messages did not convey the impression that the end was near. Two hours afterwards the announcement came that the Duke had passed away . . . (*Inverness Courier*, 23 September 1892).

He died at 10.30pm and his younger son, the Earl of Cromartie, arrived barely ten minutes after his father's death. The Duke had not been in the best of health in recent years but it was now noted that he had "failed very much of late"

(*Glasgow Herald*, 23 September 1892). It was first thought that a heart condition had caused his death and that "the illness was so short that his death might be described as sudden" (*The Times*, 24 September 1892). Rumours began to spread. It was speculated that it had been indigestion, "followed by symptoms of a grave character" and "although medical aid was at hand from an early stage . . . nothing that could be done could avert a fatal issue (*Scotsman*, 23 September 1892). Dr Worthington, the Duke's physician, who had been summoned to attend, felt compelled to write regarding "the several incorrect impressions of the Duke's illness and death (which) have appeared in the *Scotsman* and other papers". He stated "I think it desirable to put forward a correct account of his death". Dr Worthington declared "A perforated ulcer of the lower end of the stomach accounted for the sudden collapse and death" (*Glasgow Herald*, 26 September 1892). Worthington and Simpson had together performed an autopsy twelve hours after the death to establish its cause.

Not surprisingly, given the unexpectedness of his death, it was reported that "the Duchess though deeply affected bore up well" (*Glasgow Herald*, 23 September 1892). She had shown her mettle in the past; now was not the time for wilting.

Pipers played their lament, the Sutherland Volunteers formed a guard of honour and an assembled crowd of tenantry paid their respects as the coffin left Dunrobin to begin its journey by rail to Trentham. George Sutherland may have been Lord Lieutenant of the County, a Knight of the Garter, and rich and powerful, but he had also been their landlord and their friend. The words of Burns perhaps came to a few throats

> Then gently scan your brother man,
> Still gentler sister woman:
> Tho' they may gang a kennin wrang,
> To step aside is human.

It was a tearful farewell. He may have erred but he had been much liked.

The coffin of polished oak was carried into Trentham Church by estate workers and was immediately followed by the Duchess leaning on the arm of her brother Rev. Arthur Michell, after whom followed her daughter, Irene Blair, and then the Duke's sons, the Marquis of Stafford (now the new Duke) and the Earl of Cromartie, together with Henry Chaplin MP, the 3rd Duke's son-in-law and widower of Lady Florence. Sir Dighton Probyn represented the Prince and Princess of Wales but the press noted that there was "an almost total absence of titled nobility" (*Glasgow Herald*, 27 September 1892).

The Prince and Princess also sent a wreath. The wreath from the Duchess bore the letter 'S' in Neapolitan violets and the attached card simply stated "With a wife's undying love".

The body was then laid to rest in the family mausoleum. For the Duke the battle was over. He was at peace. For the Duchess the battle lay ahead. There would be no peace.

CHAPTER TWELVE

Family At War

Where shall the lover rest,
Whom the fates sever
From his true maiden's breast,
Parted for ever?
SIR WALTER SCOTT – from *Marmion*

As long as the Duke lived, there remained a glimmer of hope that reconciliation between him and his children might be possible. Dead and gone, however, no such possibility existed. At the funeral the Duchess and the Sutherlands did not even exchange glances let alone utter words of condolence. The acrimony between the new Duke and the widow of the 3rd Duke was not to be buried beside his remains in the grand yet grim mausoleum at Trentham. Instead it was destined to grow and flourish.

There was ample reason for war gaining momentum. The late Duke's will was unacceptable to the new Duke. As his solicitors have noted

> it is difficult to imagine a Will less in keeping with the spirit of the times, or more calculated to inflame feelings of distaste and mistrust. The benefits given to the Duchess by the Will and Codicil were so extensive that it looked as though those documents might almost have been written at her dictation. Indeed her stepson suspected that they had been. (Drummond, 1982, 30).

In effect, both Will and Codicil gave the Dowager a huge slice of the Duke's personal fortune and control over much of the remainder. She was to get £100,000 in cash and an annuity

of £9,000 together with almost all the non-heirloom items of
the stately homes and near countless other items. Even
Duchess Blair's daughter Irene was to benefit to the tune of
£12,000 while nothing was earmarked for the Duke's own
children.

It was a will that almost demanded to be fought over. Battle
soon commenced.

By 7 October the press was able to tell of "serious family
broils". The Dowager-Duchess arrived in London after a visit
to Staffordshire and was driven to a West End hotel where
she proposed to remain for some time, the object of her stay
being to consult her solicitors and at some length. The new
Duke had prevented her from gaining entry to Tittensor
Chase for he had put his men in possession. It was also stated
that "he had lost no time in accepting charge of the Trentham
Estate (where) nearly all the servants have been re–instated"
(*Evening Times*, 7 October 1892). It was announced the Duke
would contest the will. The Dowager, on the other hand,
intended contesting her stepson's actions over Tittensor
which her late husband had leased to her in his lifetime and
confirmed in his will.

The Sutherland Will Case promised to be one of the most
exciting legal tussles of the century and there would be rich
pickings to be had in this financial battle.

Although Mary Caroline had been given some jewellery in
the will and given the famous Sutherland Jewels for her "use
and enjoyment during her life", subject to some security being
offered, it was not to be so straightforward. One of the
trustees of the Sutherland Estates, the Duke of Westminster,
quickly acted to get the courts to establish that many of the
jewels were heirlooms and belonged to the estate. The case
came before Mr Justice North on 9 December 1892. The
Dowager-Duchess stated that some of the jewels were lodged
with her bank while others were at Stafford House or
Tittensor Chase and she could only get them if she had access
to these houses. Justice North did not rise to the bait – he
instructed her to place the jewels currently with the bank in

the hands of the Court and that she prepare an affidavit as to where the other jewels were located. Thus some of the jewels slipped through her hands. She had lost the first skirmish. It perhaps did not augur well for the future.

A few days later Tittensor Chase itself was back on the legal agenda. The outcome of which was that Mr Justice North refused an application by the Dowager-Duchess that she be allowed to spend Christmas at the house; instead she was simply to be allowed to recover her personal property. The Duke in turn claimed he was willing to hand over to her "anything that was admittedly hers" (*Times*, 22 December 1892). Tittensor too seemed to be slipping away.

Before the end of the year Sutherland v Sutherland was before Mr Justice Jeune, President of the Probate Court. Both parties agreed that an administrator of the estate was required while the case was pending. The President made an order that if the parties could not agree as to who would act as administrator the Court would appoint one.

By the spring of 1893 the well-known surveyor, Robert George Clutton, had been appointed Administrator pendente lite to manage the estate until the will dispute was settled. On 11 March Lord President Jeune directed that boxes of papers and tables containing certain letters should be removed from Stafford House and taken to Mr Clutton's offices in Whitehall. The order had been made because the Dowager was anxious to obtain papers which were of a private character and which she believed the late Duke would have wished destroyed. On the other hand there was the possibility that letters might throw light on the litigation and the present Duke did not want any such papers destroyed. It was thus deemed desirable and in both parties' interests to inspect the papers together.

In the office of Mr Henry Clutton, brother of the Administrator and a solicitor, there gathered the solicitors to both parties and the three executors of the will. Mr Clutton explained the purpose of the meeting and stressed the need for care in handling the documents and that any letters she

wished destroyed were to be handed to him and they would
then be placed in sealed packets and offered to the Duke for
his inspection. Thus in front of the group her examination of
the papers began. The Duchess soon became quite agitated
and complained that some papers were not as they had been
when she had last seen them. She declared that they had been
tampered with. Suddenly she picked up one paper, rose from
her chair, crossed the room to the fireplace and placed the
document between the bars of the fire. Flames immediately
consumed it – only the Duchess had been aware of its
contents, now, alas, lost forever.

The *Glasgow Herald,* has charmingly imagined the scene

> a small group of legal gentlemen all more or less
> lynx–eyed and all watching each other as the mysteri-
> ous papers are carefully untied . . . the beautiful impul-
> sive graceful elusive lady . . . succeeds in circumventing
> them all getting possession of the crucial documents
> and consigning them to the flames.

Dumbstruck, the assembled company looked in disbelief. At
last the Duke's solicitor, Mr Taylor, realising the immensity of
the act exclaimed his tardy protest, but the Duchess haughtily
retorted, "The document was a letter from me to my husband
before I was married. I shall do as I please, and you are only
here on sufferance" (*Glasgow Herald,* 19 April 1893).

It was not a statement geared to soothe a delicate, even if
inflammatory, situation let alone win friends and influence
people. As in the past her high handedness had landed her in
trouble.

Taylor proposed to have her charged with contempt of
court. She had in his view burnt a document taken from the
late Duke's papers which doubtless had an important bearing
on the litigation. There being "no smoke without fire" seems
the logical comment!

Sir Henry James QC, for the Duke, stated in court on 18 April
that she "had taken upon herself a very serious burden in
reading that document without communicating its contents to

anyone whilst it was in existence and then having destroyed it unexplained". It was his view that her "statement as to the contents of the letter could not be relied upon. Anyone who thus destroyed a document could not expect that her statement of its contents should be accepted". It was, he submitted, a matter of grave contempt of Court and asked that "His Lordship deal out justice in the case."

Mr Finlay QC, for the Dowager-Duchess, apologised profusely for her actions but also explained that she did not consider that a private letter from the Duke to herself which had somehow accidentally got mixed up with the Duke's papers to be within the scope of the order and had thus destroyed it. He then proceeded to read an affidavit by the Duchess in which she had stated

> the late Duke, a few hours before his death, gave her special instructions to take from his private drawers and boxes at Stafford House certain papers and destroy them. Among them was a letter written by the late Duke to her in the course of a yachting excursion in the winter of 1886 . . . it had nothing to do with the case and related to an unpleasant occurrence affecting other persons . . . of an especially private character (*Glasgow Herald*, 19 April 1893).

Whether the letter did indeed relate to "an unpleasant occurrence between the steward and the maid" (*The Times*, 19 April 1893) we will never know. Explaining that the destruction of something was carried out to conceal some actions of unknown others and then to offer information which though not naming them still clearly identified those involved seems a queer way to offer protection. It seemed more like just another, if rather feeble, excuse for a wrongdoing. Not surprisingly Sir Henry James protested that he could not accept her explanation.

Which of her stories was to be believed? She had originally stated the letter was from her hand but now claimed it had been written by the Duke. Liars need to have a good memory

and some consistency! No one will ever know the contents of
that letter. Who had written it and who received it are now
mysteries. The paper may probably have related to the will
but if, as 'Duchess Blair' claimed, it had been written prior to
their marriage might it have thrown light on some incident in
the past, the death of Mr Blair perhaps? Since we do not know
the contents we might reasonably speculate on the worst
possible – was it a letter of blackmail to the Duke over his
shooting of Blair? Was it a letter which incriminated Duchess
Blair in 'murder'? There is one over–riding fact – *it was a letter
so important that it had to be destroyed.* Was it destroyed in a
rash and foolish moment or was it a deliberate and carefully
engineered act of sabotage? If the latter, it would seem that if
she was prepared to commit an act so prejudicial to her own
case and at a risk of untold consequences then the document
had to be of major import. Its complete destruction was
deemed more essential than possible reprisals. That must
surely be the measure of the significance of the document.

Whether by impulse or planned deceit she had destroyed a
document. It was probably important to the case (and it
would certainly have been important to this story!). It was
indeed unforgivable.

Grim-faced, Sir Francis Jeune declared it was an act which
he considered without parallel. He believed the Court had
tried in good faith to be helpful to both parties and that she
had deliberately abused its trust. He stated "an apology could
only be regarded as a somewhat easy matter of atonement".

The President stated

> Justice must be done in this case as in any other . . . no
> Court could possibly pass by a grave contempt of its
> authority, and a grave attempt to interfere with the
> course of justice (*Glasgow Herald*, 19 April 1893).

He recalled that in a somewhat similar case a fine of £500
and sentence of three–months imprisonment had been
imposed. While believing that he did not require to go quite as
far as in that case it nevertheless gave him "some indication"

of what ought to be done. He concluded

> in his view he would be doing less than his duty if he
> did not pass an order which he was conscious was a
> severe one, but not too severe, and as lenient as he
> could bring himself consistently with his duty to make,
> and the order of the court would be that the Dowager
> Duchess be fined £250 and . . . be committed to prison
> for six weeks (*Glasgow Herald*, 19 April 1893).

Murmurs, more of sensation as much as approval or sympathy, rose from the packed galleries.

It had been a very "painful duty" (*The Times*, 10 April 1905) for Mr Justice Jeune had been a Fellow at Oxford in her father's old College and his father too had been the Master of an Oxford College. He had known old Dr Michell and liked him – he had some empathy towards his daughter. But Jeune could not let personal views impede his judicial qualities of uprightness and impartiality. "Justice must be done".

One of the correspondents covering the case has painted a graphic picture of the Dowager-Duchess. She is described as

> . . . a splendid looking woman with a masterful will,
> rare power of self-control, and a voice and variety of
> facial expressions which are seldom found off the stage
> (*Evening Times*, 19 April 1893).

The *Daily Mail* cheekily suggested

> The whole incident seems to suggest that a new imple-
> ment must be added to the scanty furniture of a solici-
> tor's office. The custodians of papers which are offered
> for perusal should hold them firmly with a pair of
> tongs (*Evening Times*, 19 April 1893).

The Duchess, accompanied by a gentleman (doubtless her solicitor, George Lewis), entered the carriage waiting for them at the Carey Street entrance. The press assumed she was being taken direct to Holloway Jail. The Duchess had other ideas.

CHAPTER THIRTEEN

A Penal Interlude –
Holloway Holiday

Mrs BARTON: That sounds like nonsense, my dear.
Mr BARTON: May be so, my dear; but it may be a very good law
for all that.
SIR WALTER SCOTT – from *Guy Mannering*

Although she had borne up well after the indignity of being sentenced to six weeks imprisonment, the Dowager-Duchess broke down when she reached her home, the Willows, in Windsor. She was compelled to take to her bed. As the night progressed her condition became much worse and her maid summoned Dr Francis Worthington early the next morning. It was diagnosed that she was "suffering from severe nervous depression and the shock resulting from the mental strain which she had endured the previous day" (*The Times*, 20 April 1893). Little improvement was noted when Dr Samuel Wyburn visited her later in the day and he confined her to bed.

The order for her committal to prison had been drawn up and placed in the hands of the court official for its implementation. The Dowager-Duchess was, however, clearly so indisposed that she could not travel and give herself up in London.

She telegraphed the authorities telling them of her inability to surrender to them and dispatched her brother, Rev. Arthur Michell, to London with her medical certificates to prove the point. By the time he had reached London the Tipstaff had already left for Windsor to arrest the Duchess.

On his arrival at the Willows the Tipstaff was shown copies of the certificates and thus he had no alternative but to return to London alone. The press intimated that the Dowager-Duchess hoped to travel to London as soon as her health permitted but that an application for her release on health grounds would be lodged.

On Thursday she made some recovery and her doctors allowed her to rise from her sick bed but during the night the doctors were hastily summoned for she was found to be lying in an unconscious state on her sofa. After medication she recovered a little and was able to pass a more comfortable night than was supposed possible and she was considerably improved by the time the doctors returned in the morning.

It transpired that she had been an invalid for some time and had been suffering "from a weak heart and other troubles" (*The Times*, 22 April 1893) and her doctors advised against her going to London but as she felt a little better she was now eager to get the ordeal underway. She now declared her willingness to surrender to the Tipstaff. The arrest "was effected very quietly in the evening" noted *The Times*, although it had been intimated to the Duchess, in the afternoon, that the very arrival of the Tipstaff had signalled her arrest.

About 6 o'clock the Dowager-Duchess entered the drawing room perfectly calm and collected. She coldly eyed Mr Hawkins, the Tipstaff, as he read the order of the court to which she simply responded with an "Oh yes, Oh yes," and then rose from her chair to make some last minute preparations. She was not one to rush. Nevertheless she was soon ready, and accompanied by Dr. Worthington, the Tipstaff, her maid and a pile of luggage she was driven in a close carriage to Slough Railway Station, shortly after 6.30 pm. From there she and her companions caught the 7.10 train to London. Few other passengers were on the platform and thus her departure went almost unnoticed. She looked pained and glum – it is not often a Duchess embarks on a journey to prison. Not surprisingly it has been said that she had "the air of a Christian virgin going to her martyrdom" (Stuart, 1982, 44).

At Westbourne Park Station she was met by her brother and some friends and after bidding goodbye to her friends she went, with her brother and travelling companions, in a horse-drawn carriage with coachman in livery to Holloway. She might be going to gaol but she was still the Duchess of Sutherland! Although pale and tired she seemed to be in much better health than she had been earlier in the week.

As the coach drew near she permitted herself a glance at the principal front of Holloway as its tall battlemented towers now loomed up before her. She frowned, for Holloway Castle, although modelled on Warwick Castle, seemed rather grim and depressing. It was not the sort of place where one would choose to spend time. With any luck her stay there would be short, and the shorter the better. She imagined it most likely her sentence would be cut short as soon as her solicitors' appeal was accepted.

Holloway, opened in 1852 as 'The House of Correction' for the City of London, had been built in the countryside. Forty years on, however, London had encroached. Some houses had been built to within 100 feet of the prison's 18 feet high brick wall and some of their windows afforded such a magnificent view of the women prisoners that the wall had to be raised by another 3'6" to thwart the attentions of Peeping Toms.

On arrival at the prison the carriage waited until the iron gates unceremoniously opened and it hastily entered and soon hooves and wheels noisily clattered across and reverberated round the inner courtyard and as it approached the great iron barred doors of the main block they too immediately opened. She did not even notice the great stone Gryphons on their pedestals on either side of the door as the carriage entered. In the mythological past Gryphons had guarded Grecian gold mines but these were simply mute sentinels guarding over 450 prisoners housed in the cells within. Inside the coach drew level with the reception door and the Duchess alighted in silence and was received by the Chief Warder, William Hugget, and the prison medical officers, Doctors Gilbert and Pitcairn.

It was a rather an impatient and unsmiling reception committee. She had apparently been expected at 6 o'clock and yet had not arrived until 8.40 pm. With a veneer of politeness and pretence of patience they received the Duchess into their care. It was a rare if rather unpleasant duty and had she not looked so glum it might have been considered something of a privilege; it is not every day that one gets the opportunity to welcome a Dowager-Duchess to prison. The Duchess looked pale and miserable.

The social reformers Beatrice and Sydney Webb considered that the Prison Commissioners prescribed a uniformity of treatment for all prisoners which comprised cellular isolation, absolute non intercourse among prisoners, the rule of silence, oakum-picking, and the tread-wheel. The press had speculated that "her Grace will be treated in the same fashion as ordinary prisoners committed for contempt of court". The regime was for

> prisoners of this class who elect to provide themselves with food, a common room is allotted during the day, and in this apartment her Grace will be compelled to associate with women committed from the County Courts. As the regulation permitting prisoners to furnish and pay for the use of private cells is abolished, her Grace will be compelled to occupy an ordinary cell provided with metal wash basin, table, chair and small iron bedstead. She will be expected to do her share of cleaning, although she may be relieved from this by arrangement with one of her companions (*Evening Times*, 19 April 1893).

The report contained some words of caution, however, for it added "unless it is otherwise ordered". It was to be otherwise ordered. That was not how it was to be for the Duchess. As a Chancery prisoner it was considered that she should be permitted certain little 'luxuries'.

She was taken to F Wing on the east side which was the female wing of the prison and from there to her cell. It is perhaps little wonder that the press referred to it as a "cell" in inverted commas for it was no ordinary prison cell. A chamber in Warwick Castle could scarcely have been more comfortable. It was a roomy apartment of about twenty–five feet long by fifteen feet wide. It had been fitted up "in very comfortable style" (*The Times*, 22 April 1893) by Maples, the furniture dealers, who had delivered the furniture in two vans early in the afternoon. The chairs were of blue plush material and a fine carpet graced the floor with tapestries taking away any austerity from the walls. A brass bedstead with adjacent toilet suite stood in one corner and the room's fire was now adorned by having a bright fender and irons – all of which "added to the cheerful appearance of the room". *The Times* also pointed out that "additional comforts (were) presumably contained in a number of trunks conveyed in a small wagonette which was kept outside until long after her Grace had been received into prison" (*The Times*, 2 April 1893). The Duchess with her lady-like tastes had transformed a bleak cell into a Lady's boudoir.

Reporters delighted to tell that some well-known confectioners would cater for the Duchess during her detention as long as the prison authorities did not object but it certainly seemed as though the visiting justiciaries had indeed "made special relaxation of the rules in her favour" and that she would be able to use her own plate, drink her own wines, receive her friends and read newspapers and books. All that she was denied was freedom.

One MP was alarmed at what seemed special privileges and the relaxation of prison regulations and asked the Home Secretary if these same indulgences were afforded to all prisoners "committed as first-class misdemeanants". It certainly seems to have been a fairly standard practice. The prison by the late nineteeenth century had acquired the nickname 'Cabmans' Castle' with its more distinguished prisoners having "food brought to them by their 'lackeys' in Hansom Cabs and who were at liberty to draw upon the services of the nearest upholsterers" (Oliver, 1990, 4). Eating houses had been set up outside the gates so that food could be ordered and this depending on status "was brought in tins, basins or red 'kerchiefs' ("Oliver" 1990, 8) so the Duchess acquiring her food from the likes of Harrods was only a slightly more extravagant abuse of a widespread indulgence. The Duchess was ever one to go over the top. A later prisoner who seems to have been subjected to somewhat similar treatment was Oscar Wilde. A report of his stay tells that the "eminent litter-ateur" could be seen "warming his soup over the cell fire, while his proofs lay on his handsome writing desk waiting collection by his lawyers" (Oliver, 1990, 8).

Application was rapidly made for the Duchess's release on the grounds of ill–health. On the morning of 5 May Sir Francis Jeune, President of the Probate and Divorce Division, took his seat in dignified silence and listened earnestly and patiently as the Duchess's Counsel read four affidavits stating that the Dowager-Duchess's health had suffered and would continue to suffer from further continuance in prison. Three of the doctors (Dr Nunn of Middlesex Hospital and Drs Wyburn and Worthington of Windsor) had for some time attended the Duchess and were aware of her state of health. Chiefly her medical problems were a weak heart and poor circulation and they were now concerned about her health in prison. Dr Philip Gilbert of Holloway had met the Duchess for the first time on her entry to gaol and when she had been weighed at that time she had been 12st 2lb, whereas now she was but 11st. and had been under his medical care while in Holloway. He too was concerned for her well-being and concluded his statement by saying

> . . . I attribute this difference to her imprisonment. She has taken but very little nourishment, and . . . is suffer-ing severely in her health from the said imprisonment.

> In my judgement . . . further imprisonment may be
> permanently injurious to her health, and might produce
> serious consequences (*The Times*, 6 May 1893).

The Duchess's Counsel having presented these affidavits
asked for remission of her sentence. After a brief dialogue on
whether the President had the power to alter a sentence once
pronounced the judgement was given. Although all four affidavits had been similar – it would have been difficult to imagine four statements quite so alike – Sir Francis, renowned for
giving attentive hearing to both sides, had chosen not to
recognise the evidence apparently so strongly weighted in the
Duchess's favour and instead (perhaps with some justification) paid particular heed to the affidavit of Dr Guiness who
had been ordered by the Home Office to carry out a medical
examination of the Duchess and whose views clearly ran
counter to the four. The Judge therefore stated that he
believed the statements to be "differing in their language and
markedly differing in their view" (*The Times*, 6 May 1893). He
thus concluded in his familiar serious and scholarly tones,
washing his hands of the whole affair, that he had "no opinion as to whether ground is made out for releasing the
Duchess . . . I think it best that the whole matter should be
dealt with without prejudice by the Home Secretary". It may
have been a sound and even shrewd judgement but it was not
a very compassionate one.

George Lewis, the Duchess's solicitor went to Holloway and
told her the result of the court's deliberations. The outcome of
it all was that the Home Office declined to accept the application for release. The sentence had to run its course. No further
serious health problem affected her stay at Holloway. Perhaps
she became resigned to her lot – no further loss of weight was
reported. But no matter the state of health, more seriously, her
pride had been severely wounded.

Thus on Monday 29 May 1893 on the expiration of her six
weeks in detention Her Grace left Holloway at 8.30 am, very
quietly.

She may not have been treated like a common criminal but

she had nonetheless been treated like a criminal. Wounded pride and annoyance hastened her into the cab without a smile and without taking the opportunity to savour the first taste of freedom. She did not look back – it had been a painful experience and one best put behind her. It would never be forgotten.

Paradoxically, the Earl and Countess of Warwick left the real Warwick Castle, to go to Elmhurst Hall, near Lichfield, to stay with the Duke of Sutherland and his wife, on the very day the Dowager-Duchess was released from Holloway Castle. The Prince of Wales was later to arrive as guest at Lichfield – Daisy Warwick was not only half sister to Millicent, Duchess of Sutherland, but was the current Mistress of the Prince of Wales.

No doubt because of the time of day – 8.30 being a time when all London would be up and about – she desired to travel quietly, so she went by road to Windsor rather than take the train. It was shortly after noon when she arrived at the welcoming wonderful Willows. Never had home been so good.

A deputation of her friends arrived in the early afternoon intending to present her with a token of their sympathy on her home-coming but she was too tired to receive them. Instead, it was intimated to them that she hoped to see them all before long. Her friends therefore handed over to her private secretary a handsome solid silver casket which contained £250 in five £50 notes.

The following inscription surmounted by a ducal crown had been engraved upon the lid of the casket:

> This casket (with £250, the amount of the fine imposed) was presented, on the 29th May, 1893, to Mary Caroline Duchess of Sutherland, by a number of sympathising English and Scotch friends, as an expression of indignant protest against the severe order by a Judge for having unflinchingly carried out a dying request of her husband.

She may have regained the money but six weeks out of her life had been lost forever. No amount of sympathy would ever restore the missing hours.

The Duchess, however, made no complaint with regard to her treatment in prison and doubtless considered that the officials at Holloway had been fair and kind to her. It had nonetheless been an ordeal and she had lost over one stone in weight. No amount of letters and flowers (and there had been hundreds of them) could restore the hurt pride at being incarcerated in Holloway Castle. It had not been too unpleasant but it had been no holiday.

CHAPTER FOURTEEN

'With The Best Will
In The World'

Vengeance, deep–brooding o'er the slain,
Had lock'd the source of softer woe;
And burning pride and high disdain
Forbade the rising tear to flow.
SIR WALTER SCOTT – from *The Lay of the Last Minstrel*

With the Duchess's jail experience behind her the legal battles of Sutherland v. Sutherland resumed.

The hearing concerning the country-house known as Tittensor Chase was the first to hit the headlines. Tittensor Chase, an attractive black and white Tudor house of 1856 vintage, had been leased to the Duchess in 1889 under a twenty-one year lease. She had, more recently, also leased a piece of adjacent land under a ninety-nine year lease. Both leases had been confirmed by the will of her husband the late Duke. Her stepson had however denied her access to the property and the Court had earlier refused to allow her to take control of it.

The Dowager-Duchess now desired to recover possession. She was furious about the Duke's refusal to yield and his tactics to thwart her occupancy. She now wanted the Court to ensure that he and his agents refrain from entering and trespassing on her holdings. She had been incensed by the last decision. Surely this time they would see sense and confirm her legal rights?

She had not much cared for Mr Justice North or his justice.

He had a reputation for being slow, narrow and fussy. It was claimed he had been "the last man in the world to seek popularity" (*The Times*, 14 October 1913). He was decidedly unpopular with the Duchess. She was glad he now had other cases to try. "Good luck to them: good riddance to him" she perhaps mused, "Another judge; another day". Now she might see some justice.

In mid-June 1893 the hearing in the Chancery Court commenced. At the end of ten days Mr Justice Romer delivered his verdict. He stated in solemnly measured tones that in his judgement the two leases which had been the subject of the action could not stand. He believed the 3rd Duke, in granting the leases at Tittensor, had not done so in the interests of his family, instead, in the Justice's assessment, the Duke had leased

> . . . for the purpose of conferring . . . a benefit upon his wife . . . at the expense or to the serious injury of those who were to come after him under the settlement in the enjoyment of the estate (*Glasgow Herald*, 22 June 1893).

He concluded by declaring that it seemed

> ". . . the Duke granted the leases in a moment of spleen – for the purpose of spiting his descendants. He acted not only illegally but blindly in a moral sense. The judgement of the Court was simply a vindication of outraged justice" (*Evening Times*, 22 June 1893).

The action was thus "dismissed with costs".

The Dowager's heart missed a beat. Had she heard correctly? She had listened intently – there could be no mistake. Tittensor Chase was not to be hers after all! Not only was she not gaining the leases but had to pay for that privilege. Justice? She almost wished Lord North had been present – he simply dithered and delayed, Lord Romer came to painful decisions.

The *Evening Times* (22 June 1893) added its view on the matter: "The Dowager-Duchess may appeal but unless Mr

Justice Romer is wrong in law she cannot possibly succeed". There was to be no appeal. Tittensor Chase was definitely not to be hers. On the legal battlefield she had been badly bruised. She might be down, but she was not out.

These cases, however, had been sideshows – it was the event in the big ring that mattered. Being beaten in the scraps may not bode well for the main contest but it does not make it a foregone conclusion. In the past she had under-estimated the forces lined against her and over-estimated her own strengths. The grand strategy needed to be re-assessed.

She must now look elsewhere for her Dower House. She had been frustrated in having the property which she had regarded as rightfully hers. She must now ensure that she could obtain a worthy and suitable alternative. She *would* have a great house. Nothing must now get in the way. She thus became all the more determined to take every penny she could from the Sutherland Estate. That would be the one sure way to have the Dower House of her dreams. Settling the Will to her satisfaction would enable that dream to become reality. The Battle for the Will would be the decisive battle in the campaign. It would provide the key to the new Dower House of Sutherland.

Although the legal battles were to be largely fought in the Probate Court in London, they were not limited to that arena. In the Court of Session in Edinburgh a minor skirmish took place in November 1893 when petitions were presented to charge the Duke's estate with expenses for improvements carried out by the late Duke. An administrator of the Scottish estates, Mr Donald Mackenzie, had been appointed in the spring, but it was resolved that no decision could be reached until matters were settled in the English courts. Though a bit of a legal non-event, the Edinburgh case did, however, allow for the introduction of Edward Salvesen QC, Counsel for the Dowager-Duchess, into our proceedings, Salvesen was to become a distinguished High Court Judge as well as a lover of the Scottish countryside and he would become an important figure in a later part of this saga.

The death of the Earl of Cromartie on 24 November 1893, at the early age of forty-one, caused a flurry of diversionary excitement for he left no male heir and there was concern, had it been a British peerage, that it might lapse. Queen Victoria had bestowed the title upon his mother and it was probably also a revival of an old Scottish peerage so it was perhaps a needless flap – the title did pass to his eldest daughter and the line flourishes to this day.

It was to be some months before the Sutherland Will Case re-appeared in Court. The Duke's QC had been promoted to Lord of Appeal and thus had to retire from his brief. When it was eventually scheduled for hearing other cases ran on and further delayed its arrival. The case of Hopegood v French might be interesting enough but it was holding up the case everyone wanted to hear about. *The Times* stressed its magnitude – "if fought out, the case promises to be one of the longest and costliest will cases ever tried in the Probate Court" (21 May 1894).

On 7 June 1894 the case came on for hearing. The Court rapidly filled and the front bench was laden with piles of legal documents and books on law. Sir Francis Jeune, President of the Probate Court, took his seat at 10.35 and Sir Edward Clarke QC, Counsel for the Duke, soon rose to ask the Judge for postponement for fifteen minutes. A buzz of excited conversation filled the Court. The quarter of an hour stretched endlessly.

Spectators may have sensed something was afoot due to the continuing absence of learned counsel and when they did re-appear it was all sadly over. After an hour's waiting the doors opened. At twenty-five past twelve the Dowager-Duchess, dressed in black as if in mourning, entered the court accompanied by her friend Mrs Mackenzie, wife of the Sheriff at Dornoch, and her maid, amid a renewed flutter of excitement. The sense of drama heightened.

The Duke of Sutherland and his brother-in-law, Henry Chaplin, entered and sat next to their Counsel. The President took his seat. Sir Henry James QC, for the Duke, rose to his feet and declared that it gave him great pleasure to announce an "arrangement" had been made and thus Judge and jury could be relieved. Sir Richard Webster QC, for the Dowager-Duchess, simply added that "proceedings have been withdrawn . . . the Dowager-Duchess no longer desires to be involved in the administration of the estate" (*Scotsman*, 8 June 1894).

It had all been agreed behind closed doors – there were to be no titillating revelations: dirty linen was not gaining a public airing. The crowded court and the anxious public outside were all to be disappointed in the extreme. While the *Glasgow Herald* (8 June 1894) might believe "the chagrin which this abrupt and unexpected dénouement may produce in the minds of the public will be something of momentary duration" at that moment there was nothing but a feeling of emptiness and sense of loss.

The Judge called for Mr John Culverwell, the witness to the signing of the Duke's Will, and he was asked to verify the circumstances and the signature. In response to the question "During that time was the Duke in sound mind and understanding?" Culverwell replied "I should think so" and laughter erupted in court. Mr Macauley, the Duke's Golspie solicitor, was then asked to verify the circumstances of the Codicil. He explained how he had been summoned to Dunrobin on 22 September 1892 and had been instructed to draw up a Codicil to the Will and this he had done. He confirmed that Dr Worthington had acted as witness.

That was the rather dully routine extent of the formality – the will was proved. That was an end to it.

There was no explosion. It had been defused. The case had ended not with the expected bang but with a whimper. A damp squib had been substituted for a display of fireworks.

Mr Justice Jeune had tried many cases in his distinguished career but this had been unique. Ever learned and lucid with a serious air, he was the complete professional. He had remained unruffled, dignified and completely impartial giving every consideration to both sides although his courte-

ousness and patience had been sorely tried. The case had had
its amusing undercurrents but he had discouraged flippancy
and steered it to sensible outcome, stalemate giving way to
settlement.

His Lordship stated

> I am very glad the parties have come to an arrange-
> ment. I think it is wise to have done so. It has been a
> great saving of public time and, probably, a great
> saving of expense . . . Whenever it is possible . . . it is
> extremely desirable that matters which are painful, or
> might be painful, to discuss in public, that the public
> discussion should be avoided (*Scotsman*, 8 June 1894).

The case has been well assessed thus

> had (it) opened the best forensic talent at the Bar would
> have been unsparingly devoted to secure the success of
> either side . . . they have better served their clients by
> preventing the case being heard at all. (*Evening Times*, 8
> June 1894).

Not only had the settlement meant a saving in time and
money but it chiefly represented a great saving in public soul-
bearing. One paper sensibly declared

> We have no knowledge of the precise issues that would
> have been raised . . . but actions of this character are
> seldom fought out to the bitter end without disclosing
> family differences far better kept private, which are apt
> to be intensified if not rendered permanent with public-
> ity (*Glasgow Herald*, 8 June 1894).

Quite why or how the will settlement was reached remains
a mystery. We will probably never know. Rumour had it that
a person "high in the State" (*Glasgow Herald*, 8 June 1894) had
intervened and the most likely candidate seemed to be the
Prince of Wales.

Writing about the Prince and his interest and support for his
then mistress, Lillie Langtry, it had been noted that "he could

always be relied upon to exert a little pressure here and to use a little influence there" (Aronson, 1988, 99). This would likely have been true of his actions in other matters and particularly in the affairs of the Duke of Sutherland and the increasingly bitter squabble with the Dowager-Duchess. The former was his friend and the latter, even if she were not one of the Prince's intimates, would be known to him and was the widow of one of his closest friends. The Prince's mistress, Daisy Brooke, was the half-sister of the present Duchess of Sutherland. The Prince had been deeply involved in the family and his deep sense of loyalty to both protagonists may well have made it personally desirable to ensure that as amicable a settlement as possible be reached as quickly as possible.

The Dowager had suffered defeat in the past – was this another defeat? She had fought valiantly – was she victorious? If she herself was not the victor, and it is difficult to see how it cannot be so construed, then it was certainly peace with honour. She had not been beaten. She was not the only victor. It most certainly must be seen as a great victory for common-sense.

How then had she gained this reversal in fortune?

More ruthless tactics had been required. In military parlance she had been compelled, as much figuratively as literally, to fight fire with fire. The opposition had been strong and perhaps they had been lulled into a false sense of security for she would be no pushover. It was then a man's world with few rights for women and in a sense she was taking on the whole might of the Establishment but fight on she would. She had probably the major weapon in the armoury for she had obtained the services of a master-craftsman. With George Lewis on her side she had the whip hand.

Without doubt the man who did the actual arranging was the Dowager-Duchess's solicitor George Lewis. He had become well-known in the influential and noble circle with a great reputation and rich clientele. He was a renowned 'fixer' and had made his name and his fortune by using his talents and persuasive skills to smooth down scandal and get things settled out of court. He had a genius for compromise. For twenty-five years or more Messrs Lewis and Lewis held the monopoly of cases involving the seamier side of Society's life but though Lewis was involved in almost every *cause célèbre* which exposed the sins and weaknesses of the affluent it was for the cases, which by his adroit handling were kept out of court, that he gained his real renown.

It was said of him that he was not so much a lawyer "as a shrewd private enquiry agent; audacious, playing the game often in defiance of the rules, and relying on his audacity to carry him through" (*The Times*, 8 December 1911). He was quite fearless and had an unrivalled knowledge of the goings-on in High Society as well as in the criminal underworld. George Smalley of the *New York Daily Tribune* has stated that Lewis "had methods of investigation which were his own, and intuitions beside which the rather mechanical processes of Sherlock Holmes seemed like a beginner".

With his sable coat and prematurely grey hair he cut a dash in London society and with panache cut a swathe through the legal jungle. In court he was always thoroughly prepared, leaving no room for surprise tactics by the opposition. His searching and ruthless cross-examination was masterful and with an encyclopaedic memory for the minutest of details notes were reduced to a minimum. He was a man to be feared.

It was said that he knew "so many of Society's secrets that he dared not keep a diary" (Brough, 1975, 248). Had he kept a diary the tasks of historians might have been immeasurably simpler! It would also have been great fun to read. Smalley believed his papers would have been enough to compromise half London and scandalise the other half. Some time before his death he had declared that all the old records of his experiences had been destroyed and no doubt a few sighs of relief in a few bedchambers resulted from that news.

Lewis was a popular dinner guest with his fund of legal tales about clients whom he did not name, delighting avid listeners who hoped that some minor misdiscretion at least might fall from his lips. In this too he was shrewd – nothing was revealed. Real clients were protected and prospective clients were amused and impressed.

Although he undoubtedly incurred fierce resentment by those he opposed, to his friends he was loyal and generous. He had long been a close friend to the Prince of Wales. In 1892 he had received a knighthood and at King Edward VII's coronation his friend awarded him with a baronetcy.

The Will settlement can be briefly stated – basically the Duke kept his estates and great houses intact while the Dowager took the money. *The Times* declared "both are reduced to absolute affluence" (*The Times*, 8 June 1894). Duchess Blair was reputed to have gained £500,000 and £5,000 per year by way of settlement but the historian of the Duke's solicitors believed that the sum of £750,000 or £850,000 would be nearer the mark. No matter what the actual sum was, she had walked off with a substantial fortune. In today's terms possibly it was something in the order of forty to fifty million pounds.

With the absence of a dramatic legal battle in the courts the public's interest remained strong and there was to be endless debate about the amount of settlement. Lady Paget's view on the Dowager-Duchess was that "her rapacity . . . was quite boundless" and in her view she had received "a million of money" (Paget, 1923, 539). Another and later estimate, from a Sutherland official, put it about that she, by the end of the day, had received two million pounds (*Northern Times*, 4 July 1935). (That might be about one hundred million pounds in today's money.)

The simple fact is that all we have is rumour and speculation.

It was also rumoured that since she had been required to quit Dunrobin Castle and was being denied a Dower House in Sutherland or indeed on any of the Sutherland's estates that the family would build her a suitable house elsewhere to her design and specification. This seems a most unlikely scenario.

Surely the Sutherland family would wish a one-off full and final settlement rather than a prolonged agony? Their desire must have been to end the business and have nothing further to do with her rather than be prepared to write a blank cheque for her building aspirations. In their view she had tried to take them to the cleaners once – would they permit a legalised rape?

No matter what was secretly agreed one fact remains – settlement was reached.

Why was this? Compromise can only be possible when two sides see greater benefit in reaching agreement than in continuing the struggle. Did Duchess Blair (or Lewis) have information concerning the present Duke or his mother (Duchess Anne) which the Duke did not wish revealed? According to Lady Paget if the case had not been stopped it would have been one of the scandals of the century for "the other side were going to bring in poor Duchess Annie's name" (*Northern Times*, 4 July 1935). Was that the only reason or did they know something about Duchess Blair's past which may have been incriminating? Was there an aspect of the 3rd Duke's life that both considered desirable to conceal? Somebody or something feared exposure. It had been the Duke's Counsel who had asked for the postponement – had they also done the yielding? Was there some substance to Lady Paget's claim?

While Holmes has remarked only when "you have eliminated the impossibilities, whatever remains, however improbable, must be the truth", in a factual account there is little to be gained by idle speculation. The facts were not revealed then and they remain obscure now. Oh, to have been able to see Lewis's japanned boxes. What dark secrets would they have revealed?

The Duchess had been bought off – it would seem she had won and handsomely. She might not have gained Sutherland but she had a huge fortune with which to indulge herself as well as, if rumours are to be believed, possibly the opportunity of having a real Dower House built at others' expense. Cheated out of Tittensor Chase she now had the wherewithal to embark on getting the Dower House of her dreams. She had now money almost "beyond the dreams of avarice". There was almost nothing she could not now afford.

Lest the reader be tempted to shed a tear for the host of legal talent appointed to contest the case and now rendered unemployed and facing loss of possible earnings, the *Evening Times* had this to say

> The settlement of the case is, of course, a pecuniary loss to these gentlemen, for it was expected to last for a fortnight. But the cloud has a double silver lining. In the language of the late Baron Huddleston "the briefs were delivered", and the fees marked on them were peculiarly substantial (8 June 1894).

It seems then that the Duchess as well as the legal profession had come out of it all with a smile on their faces.

Although the settlement had been seen as good sense reached amicably – that had been window dressing for general consumption. It was probably not swallowed by the public or the press. There had been too much bitterness for amity to suddenly reign. Family differences had hardened in the heat of battle. They had agreed peace terms not agreed to be friends.

The money had to be paid in notes – she would not accept their cheque. She had found the Duke of Sutherland to be untrustworthy in the past; why trust him now? Arrangements had to be made with the Bank of England for the special issue of bank notes of £1,000 each. David Drummond of Messrs Taylor and Humbert (the Duke's solicitors) has described the process of payment –

> . . . shortly after the settlement of the action, Ernest Humbert, wearing his invariable outfit of top hat and frock coat, trotted off in a hansom cab . . . and collected the bundles of notes from the bank. On his return to Field Court, the notes were counted again, handed over to Mr Du Cane on behalf of the Duchess, and a receipt obtained in full discharge . . . The moment they had

been credited to the Duchess's account, they had served their purpose, and winged their way back to the Bank of England, that same day, for cancellation and destruction (Drummond, 1982, 340).

The battle over, wounds could be licked. It was more of an armed truce than an end of hostilities. The war may have ended and it may not have been the start of a Cold War but it was certainly the start of the cold shoulder. The Duchess had never been liked, now she was persona non grata. Hostile feelings remained even if the battle had ended. Adversaries they would remain. War by other means was the new order.

She had joined the aristocracy by marriage; now she had truly arrived at what Thomas Carlyle called "The Aristocracy of the Moneybag". She must now ensure that neither would fall from her grip. She would, no matter what, remain the Dowager-Duchess of Sutherland. But obtaining a suitably aristocratic house would now be given the highest priority.

FOOTNOTE

The Will Case and her spell in Holloway may not have been her only brush with the law or dispute with the House of Sutherland.

The well-known chronicler of Highland life, Alasdair Alpin Macgregor, has told that, when finally forced to leave Dunrobin Castle, Duchess Blair took more than was rightfully hers including the gold-plated handles from the Royal Suite. The Duke had her charged and in due course she appeared before old Sheriff Mackenzie in the Court House at Dornoch. There she is said to have received a six-month sentence. This was considered to be somewhat light and Duchess Blair was eternally grateful for such leniency. She regularly sent the Mackenzie family "cast-off articles of apparel" which arrived at Tain station in a hamper. As a schoolboy Macgregor had been waiting for the train to Ardgay when one such hamper "stuffed to overflowing" lay on the platform and he and his schoolmates decided to amuse themselves by dressing up in the garments protruding from its sides. He must have been a pretty sight as he had pulled on, over his kilt, a pair of the Duchess's white knickers. When chased by one of the station staff the bloomers slipped to his ankles and he fell headlong onto the platform. He was caught and had his backside skelped. One suspects there was to be no more cross-dressing at Tain Station!

It is not possible to confirm or even add to the story. Having, however, examined the Dornoch Sheriff Court records in the Scottish Record Office (West Register House) no trace of an appearance let alone of a sentence of the Duchess could be found. The records of nearby Tain were also examined and to no avail. Whether she was tried elsewhere or it was another civil action, perhaps held in camera, we do not know and a dearth of press reportage makes further search well nigh impossible.

Whether there was in fact another legal battle remains a bit of a problem. We lack facts. Was this Dornoch affair a piece of half remembered or half imagined episode from the past? Was a much publicised London legal battle and Holloway incarceration simply given a little local flavour when it was recounted at the Macgregor fireside at Cnocnanoine? We may never know. Certainly Mrs Mackenzie was to become a great friend of the Duchess and it is entirely possible that aristocratic cast-offs made their way to the Mackenzie household. For Alasdair Alpin Macgregor the frilly knickers were real enough.

CHAPTER FIFTEEN

A New Romance –
A Lawyer In The House

What shall be the maiden's fate?
Who shall be the maiden's mate?
SIR WALTER SCOTT – from *The Lay of the Last Minstrel*

The Dowager-Duchess of Sutherland was not to remain a widow for long. One expects she would have been considered a fair catch by any number of possible suitors but her third husband, although not "an immensely rich duke", has been rather unfairly dismissed by the historian of the 4th Duke's solicitors, as being a "mere solicitor" (Drummond, 1982, 35). The Duchess, in fact, married Sir Albert Rollit MP. He was no 'mere solicitor' – indeed, less of a 'mere solicitor' would be hard to imagine.

He was certainly a solicitor and seems to have been a highly successful one. Under his control the firm of Rollit & Son prospered and he was to become President of the Law Society and Registrar of both the County Court and the Supreme Court. He was to end his days as a Justice on the Magistrates bench for Windsor and Berkshire. A mere solicitor, indeed! It is likely that Rollit acted as the Duchess's principal legal advisor throughout her war on the Sutherland family even if it is not possible to put an exact date on their first encounter.

As a Hull man it is not surprising he should have had an interest in the sea and shipping – he owned a steamship company – which in turn led to an interest in trade and commerce. He also became an Elder Brother of Trinity House, the lighthouse providers, and rose to the rank of Lieutenant Colonel in the Submarine miners branch of the Engineers.

Politics seems to have been an early interest. He was elected to Hull City Council and served as Mayor for two terms. It was his work on the Council that earned him his knighthood in 1885. Having achieved the highest honours and power at the local level he then turned his sights to Westminster but though he had contested the local West Hull constituency victory had eluded him.

He enjoyed an affluent life-style and did much entertaining at his magnificent country home of Thwaite House, Cottingham. Peers, politicians and bishops were frequent house guests. Among them had been Joseph Chamberlain, another great municipal figure who in Westminster was an exponent of tariff reform, perhaps reflecting Rollit's interest in trade as much as high politics. Another guest was Samuel Plimsoll of Plimsoll line fame who undoubtedly mirrored Rollit's interests in shipping and safety at sea. Among the impressive list of names in his Visitors Book, one name stands out – Oscar Wilde. He had been a guest on 25 March 1884. Thwaite Hall was later to become a Hall of Residence for the University of Hull and the student magazine has rather delightfully speculated on Wilde's visit to Thwaite and mused "I suppose it is too much to wonder in whose room he slept" (*The Torch*, December 1931).

In 1886, however, Rollit achieved his ambition and was elected for Islington South and for twenty years served as its Conservative member. In the Commons he was a distinguished figure and spoke on a wide range of issues and was reputed to have had more bills passed than any other private member but he was too independent and forthright a figure to ever hold government office. His opposition to Tariff Reform lost him the seat in 1906 and he switched parties but when he attempted to win Epsom for the Liberals in 1910 he was again defeated. It was rather a sad anti–climax to what had been a fine record of public service.

His paternal grandfather had been the Huddersfield archi-

tect and builder, Joseph Kaye, and thus it was perhaps little
wonder that he had an interest in fine buildings and had a
flair for finding property of quality. Elegant Browsholme,
near Hull, had long been his home but latterly his principal
seat was the charming St Anne's Hill, Chertsey. He was later
to lease the 2,400 acre estate of Manar, three and a half miles
west of Inverurie on the north bank of the Don. It was an ideal
spot in which a busy London solicitor could relax.

Rollit's most controversial public act was as Special
Commissioner appointed to investigate an incident at
Featherstone Colliery, near Wakefield, when troops, ordered
by Home Secretary Asquith, opened fire and killed two
miners. The Commission was widely criticised for its conclusion that the use of troops and their action had been justified.
Beyond that rather ignominious claim to fame Rollit had a
remarkably good press. He was even able to redeem himself
by becoming Chairman of the London Conciliation Board and
was for long active in endeavouring to improve industrial
relations. Sadly, records of Rollit's life and achievements are
rare but in his lifetime rewards, honours and honorary
degrees were showered upon him.

Rollit, by all accounts, seems to have been a well-liked and
generally much respected old chap and although he had a
forceful personality with extensive knowledge he was seldom
overbearing. He had a 'generous spirit of toleration'.
According to one Hull friend, in spite of 'all his astuteness
there was a naive side of him that attracted people. He was
very human'. All this together with his air of 'bonhomie' lent
him charm. He was most hospitable and outgoing and was
considered 'the Prince of Goodfellowship'. Perhaps the
Duchess had truly met her Prince Charming – not in a regal
sense but in a real sense.

He was a man of wide-ranging interests – shipping and
commerce, politics and local government, law and education
– but the Duchess was interested in none of these things and
in fact it is difficult to see quite where they had any shared
interests, other than a love of the 'good life'. Like the Duke he

was a man with many facets but whereas the Duke had been a man of action Rollit was a man of learning. He was an indoor man where the Duke was an outdoor one. The Duke had been a big adventurous schoolboy all his days but Rollit was ever the benign and scholarly old schoolmaster.

By November 1896 he had been a widower for over a year – his first wife Eleanor having died after a brief illness leaving him with one daughter. At the age of fifty-four he had fallen hopelessly in love. He asked the good-looking Duchess to marry him – she was a sprightly woman of forty-eight years – and to his surprise and delight she accepted his proposal and so they were to be married.

They were married in St George's Church, Hanover Square. Its most famous parishioner had been George Frederick Handel – he had advised on the suitability of the organ – and the church had long been noted for its fashionable weddings. Shelley, George Meredith, George Eliot and Disraeli were married there. The future American President, Theodore Roosevelt, as well as the future British Prime Minister, H. H. Asquith, were later to be married in the church. The last male heir of the old Earl of Cromartie's estates, Kenneth Mackenzie, was married in the church in 1792. It was one of *the* places to be married in. A Victorian writer considered it to be "the London temple of Hymen".

In 1896 the interior of the church, after recent refurbishment, looked splendid and on 12 November it was even more magnificent for our wedding for it had been beautifully decorated with tall palms and white chrysanthemums. The altar bore white bouquets with white blooms in the centre.

The crowd outside gasped in excitement and delight as the Duchess descended from her carriage, rested on her brother's arms and mounted the few steps between the lofty columns. She carried a bunch of orchids. It was what she wore that caught the breath of the excited onlookers – she looked wonderful in a magnificent petunia velvet gown elegantly trimmed with chinchilla fur and embroidery and studded with jewels. This was her Big Day and a day to show off some of the famous Sutherland jewels. A massive chain of diamonds sparkled richly but she also wore a splendid diamond and emerald pendant which Sir Albert had recently given to her. Her dark hair was fastened with a large diamond comb at the back.

The hushed reverence of the congregation gave way to excited chatter as the Duchess entered on the arms of her brother. They were followed by her daughter, Irene, who was wearing an ivory white gown, the skirt bordered in sable and a draped bodice of point d'Alencow lace, caught with diamond clasp and belt of brilliant scarlet velvet and carrying a bouquet of scarlet carnations. A shy grin could be discerned below the splendours of her large black velvet picture hat trimmed with scarlet feathers and sable tails. Twenty-year old girls dream of the day when they too will walk down the aisle to wed the man of their dreams. Perhaps hers would also be a knight. Or even a Duke or a Count!

One of the Duchess's nieces was the other attendant and she wore "a neat dress of white cashmere, trimmed with sable, and bonnet en suite, her nosegay being of scarlet carnations in foliage" (*Hull Daily Mail*, 13 November 1896).

The little procession appeared from below the great organ gallery and made its way slowly down the central aisle. The organ resounded in triumph. A hint of a smile appeared on the Duchess's lips as she noticed familiar faces in the pews as they craned to see her pass. Mrs Mackenzie, wife of the Sheriff, from Dornoch was there and so too was Sir Ellis Ashmead–Bartlett MP, a former Civil Lord of the Admiralty and noted Turkophile who had been imprisoned by the Greeks for his active support of Turkey.

For the most part Duchess Blair looked ahead to where Sir Albert was standing and beyond him to the magnificent mosaic of colour which is the East Window. Below the window and above the altar within the richly–carved reredos is William Kent's painting of the Last Supper but its gloomy beauties would be lost on the happy couple as they made their wedding vows at the chancel rail under the shade of the spreading palms.

The service was a fully choral one and the surpliced choir of men and boys was one of the finest of any church. The organist Charles Jolley, had come to St George's in 1892 and he was to remain there for fifty-five years maintaining high and old standards.

There were to be three clergymen officiating but her brother, Rev. Arthur Michell, took the principal part in the ceremony. It was soon over but would long be the topic of conversation.

Due to the fact that the Duchess's mother had died just a few weeks before the wedding it had been considered inappropriate to issue invitations and thus the decision had been made to have a very quiet wedding. After the service the small party returned to the Duchess's Belgrave Square house for lunch. It would also be an opportunity to admire some of the 300 presents received which the press noted were "exceptionally handsome and costly" (*Glasgow Herald*, 13 November 1896). It was a description which would have applied to the entire day – no expense had been spared; it was a day to remember. It may not have been Florida in the springtime but it was in every respect a sunny day.

Later in the afternoon Sir Albert and Lady Rollit set off for their honeymoon. It gave the Duchess another opportunity to display some of her wardrobe. Her going away outfit consisted of a grey silk velvet costume trimmed with white satin and sable and jewelled embroidery while her hat was of grey feathers and brown velvet. It would not matter that it was not colour co-ordinated and possibly rather vulgar and considerably over-the-top but it did matter that it was fancy and flamboyant. The holiday was to be spent in Spain but it had been planned to stop off in Paris en route. Paris was a firm favourite of Rollit's. He was a fluent French speaker and had many business connections with the city and had, for a time, a small apartment in Avenue d'Antin; on this occasion the best Parisian hotel would provide the bridal suite.

Married life together had got off to a colourful and happy

start. The future of St George's was not to be quite so happy.

Shortly before 11 o'clock on the evening of Wednesday 18 November passers-by noticed a strange glare in the tower of St George's but before the alarm could be raised flames had burst out and completely enveloped the tower. A large crowd gathered and they cheered the fire-engines as they arrived and police had difficulty in keeping the crowd from hindering the firefighting. It was obviously quite a sight and one can imagine the late Duke of Sutherland would have been in his element with his own fire-engine tackling the blaze but by 1896 the need for amateurs had waned and it was the professional force that soon quelled the flames. The fire may have marked the end of an epoch for St George's but the Rollit wedding may have been its swan song. The church had escaped major catastrophe. The organ had to be almost entirely rebuilt but soon all was restored to its former glory and to this day St George's flourishes as church and congregation. It is a fine church and still a truly grand place for a wedding.

CHAPTER SIXTEEN

An Illegal Interlude – The Great Jewel Robbery

And laugh'd, and shouted, 'lost! lost! lost!'
SIR WALTER SCOTT – from *The Lay of the Last Minstrel*

Paris was long to be a popular destination for Sir Albert and Lady Rollit. It was an exciting city but one particular sojourn of theirs was to be more adventuresome than others.

On the morning of 17 October 1898 Mary Caroline, Duchess of Sutherland, left her commodious suite of rooms on the first floor of the Hotel Bristol. It is a magnificent building, part of the eighteenth-century genteel elegance of the Place Vendôme, one of Paris's most delightful squares. She was returning home to England having enjoyed a five-day holiday in the French capital with her husband (Sir Albert Rollit), her brother Roland Michell, the Commissioner in Cyprus, and his wife.

As she settled down in her cab she no doubt cast an admiring glance round the square (actually an octagon) of fine buildings which had witnessed so much. There the French Emperor Napoleon III had made love to Eugenie and there Chopin had died. Her eye was again drawn to the splendid monument in the centre of the square – for Napoleon I from the top of his magnificent and lofty column dominates the scene. The Duchess perhaps mused that Napoleon had not been there when the very first Duchess of Sutherland had been in Paris. It had then been a city in the throes of revolution – a time of great fear leading in time to a greater terror, a

153

time of collapse of the Ancien Regime and a time for storming the Bastille. It had been a time for Madame Guillotine as well as Madame Defarge. The first Duchess had been eager to return to Britain and to safety for Paris had become a place of peril in 1792. A hundred years on it was simply a city of romance – a city to enjoy. In 1792 a twenty-foot statue of Louis XIV – the Sun King – astride his charger had stood in the centre of the square which then rejoiced, albeit briefly, under the name of Place de Louis le Grand but now the 144 foot high column to commemorate Napoleon's victory at Austerlitz had pride of place.

In 1870-1 the Duchess's eldest brother, Edward, had been in Paris during the siege but in 1898 Paris was a less dangerous place than it had been in 1792 or even 1871; nevertheless it was still an exciting city. The 'Naughty Nineties' were nearing their end and Toulouse-Lautrec had vividly depicted the decadence, seaminess and risqué pleasures of 'Gay Paree'. Montmartre's cafés throbbed with patrons intoxicated by the atmosphere and the alcohol. Cabarets and music halls acted as magnets to happy crowds. The frenzied milieu of the Moulin Rouge attracted an international clientele to its drinking and dancing and gave it the reputation of being *le rendez-vous du High Life*. The music of Offenbach and Gounod played to packed and enthusiastic houses. At the Folies Bergère the Can Can delighted all who came to ogle and the ballet dancers at the Opera House have been captured forever in the works of Degas. Rodin's powerful yet grotesque plaster of Balzac created a sensation and received a hostile reception at the Salon des Beaux Arts in 1898 and the Committee rejected it as the planned public memorial to the novelist. The ten year-old tower designed and built by M. Eiffel dominated the city and conversation. Work was painstakingly progressing on the Sacre Coeur – it had begun in 1876 and no end seemed to be in sight for its completion or its cost. It would not, in fact, be consecrated until 1919 and its cost estimated at over forty million francs.

In the 1890's France over-indulged herself in a love for all things English and the English in turn took Paris to their hearts. English stars topped the bills in night clubs. Tea-rooms had opened in every fashionable street. For those hungry for food as much as pleasure the Café Anglais established itself as one of the finest eating-houses in Paris and with a superb selection of French wines. Oscar Wilde, in 1898, went into exile in Paris and he almost epitomised that mixture of colour and scandal which made Paris a haven for the pleasure-seeker.

The Prince of Wales was an ardent Francophile and his bois-terous hedonistic lifestyle endeared him to the Parisian high society as well as providing a model for the English to emulate. In Paris he found a "whirl of amusements" of which he never wearied – he seemed to live purely for pleasure and Paris provided enough pleasures for a lifetime. The amorous Prince's many visits to the Jardin des Plantes was in pursuit of an interest in the female form rather than things floral. The Prince frequently stayed in the Hotel Bristol and his mistress, Daisy Warwick, was, for propriety's sake, sensibly ensconsed in the nearby Hotel Vendôme so that they could savour the joys of Paris together but maybe also so that even she did not cramp his style.

Sir Albert Rollit, as President of the Anglo-French Chamber of Commerce, was there to mix business with pleasure. The Duchess was there to enjoy herself, to shop and to ostenta-tiously display her finery. Paris was a city of showy splen-dours and she loved to show off the splendour of those Sutherland jewels. She was a lady of beauty as well as substance and wanted as much to be seen in Paris as to see Paris. For the Duchess it had been a magical if tiring few days and no dramatic incidents had marred their delightful stay in the luxury of Hotel Bristol amid the endless pleasures of Paris.

The gracious facades of the Place soon gave way to crowded streets and then the bustle and noise of the Gare du Nord. She was in ample time to catch the 11.50 train to Calais en route for London and home.

The hotel staff had doubtless attended to her every wish but to ensure she would have all the attention her status demanded the Duchess had brought her personal maid and her own footman with her to Paris. Everyone had endeavoured to ensure her stay was as trouble-free as possible.

Shortly before she left her room and having carefully laid aside the most precious of items which she would wear she and her maid, Perkins, carefully crammed her rich and dazzling collection of jewellery into the green baize-covered jewel case. She then locked it carefully and entrusted it to the maid. The Duchess looked back as she left the room. The case was on the table and Perkins had been instructed to bring it to the station. All was well; she set off for the train.

At 10.30 the servant came down the stairs nursing the jewel case and for security reasons lodged it with the porter telling him that she had to go on some errands for the Duchess but would return for it shortly. At exactly 11 o'clock she returned to collect it just as the station omnibus arrived to take her and the footman to the station. She was the last to board the vehicle and the porter handed her the case. She placed it on her knees with her hands resting on top of it. It was safe.

At Gare du Nord the footman went off to attend to the luggage while she found the first-class compartment and placed the dispatch case on the seat. Perkins watched from the train and signalled to the Duchess as soon as she was spotted coming along the platform. When the Duchess arrived she placed her purse beside the box and Perkins went off to ensure the luggage was going on board. After a few moments in the compartment the Duchess, restless as ever, stood on the platform to await the arrival of the others. When Sir Albert and Mr and Mrs Michell arrived they all boarded the train and it set off almost at once. A few minutes into the journey the Duchess searching for her handkerchief found that her purse was missing and then it was realised that the dispatch box was also missing. The compartment was thoroughly searched and to no avail – both jewel case and purse were gone. As soon as the train reached its first stop – Amiens –

Rollit and his wife left the train and having got the railway to send telegrams to police in Paris and Amsterdam as well as Scotland Yard in London they returned to Paris.

While the stationmaster at Gare du Nord, M. Cochefort, and the special police commissary there were most reticent to discuss the matter with the press the Police Commissary at Amiens was more forthcoming. He obviously believed that servants were incapable of attending to the most simple of duties and thought it possible that the jewel case might simply have been forgotten at the last moment. Presumably the missing purse with £8-£10 in it was just as forgettable. He had made enquiries by telephone and had the Duchess's rooms thoroughly searched but, of course, nothing had been found and the porter confirmed the sequence of events leading to the departure of jewel case and maid from the hotel.

The Duchess and her husband reached Paris at seven o'clock and the police informed them that everything that could possibly be done was being done. As soon as they had received information giving descriptions of the jewellery they had it circulated to jewellers and pawnbrokers and the Hotel servants had been questioned. Though they had cabled Calais, Dover and London, they had unfortunately not been in time to organise a search of passengers' luggage. It was their view that the robbery of jewels reckoned to be valued at about £25,000 – £30,000 had been "affected by expert thieves". The Paris Correspondent of *The Times* who had witnessed the departure of both party and train from the station stated that there had been "no suspicion of a robbery' at that time and as it could not be taken from a carriage containing four or five people and with no stoppages it clearly was his view that it had to have been stolen before the journey commenced. He concluded it to be "the work of professionals who must have had minute information if not accomplices" (*The Times*, 19 October 1898). The general consensus seemed to favour a gang of expert thieves as having perpetrated the crime and having had the Duchess under surveillance for days.

Perhaps already sensing the near futility of all the enquiries and despairing ever of having her beloved jewels back the Duchess offered a reward of £4000 for the recovery of her jewels. As nothing further could be gained by remaining in Paris – it no longer seemed to be quite as magical as it had been a few short hours ago – they both left barely two hours later. Home would now be very welcome indeed.

Although the police on both sides of the Channel were to continue their investigations it was in London that they were to prove most rewarding. Early in the morning of Monday 28 November Henry Williams, also known as William Johnson, was arrested by three Scotland Yard Inspectors – Dinnie, Dew and Froest – having forced their way into a house in Fulham. Williams was charged with stealing the jewellery some weeks earlier. It was reported that the officers had searched the house and found some of the missing items. Another man had also been detained but he had not been formally charged. Williams Johnson had been well known to the police and had long used several aliases, the best known one being 'Harry the Valet'.

The next day at West London Police Court William Johnson, aged forty-six and described as a dealer, and his nephew Moss Lipman, a tailor, stood in the dock. Well-known diamond merchants had identified some of the stolen property and the Dowager-Duchess was called to formally identify the few items placed before her. She had to admit tearfully that "some of the settings had been altered" and some diamonds had been taken out of clusters and set into rings but most still remained missing.

Inspector Dinnie gave evidence as to the arrest and how they had to burst open the door. Some jewellery had been found in a cash-box, some in the wardrobe and some in the drawer of the washstand. On being charged Johnson stated "If I had not been a fool and got drunk you would not have found me here". Later he was to state "women and drink" had been his downfall. (*The Times*, 30 November 1898). He had been searched and £340 in banknotes had been found in his pockets as well as some items of jewellery. Both prisoners were remanded.

When the case resumed in January 1899 there were fresh revelations as to the crime in particular and Johnson's life in general. As always in the Sutherland saga nothing was straightforward; in fact there was to be an element of mystery.

It transpired that a lady whose real identity was not revealed but referred to as Mrs Ronald was in fact "married to a gentleman of blameless character" (*The Times*, 5 January 1899) and had, in April 1898, met Johnson in a hotel in Brighton. He was to become infatuated by her. She had fallen for him so much that she went off with him and for some months they lived together in Brighton, London and in various places on the Continent. Johnson was out of work and penniless but she, being "a woman of means", supported him and gave him money. It was to be a somewhat stormy relationship and in late September they separated after a heated row, the last of numerous bitter quarrels.

She then heard nothing further from him until after the robbery when she received a letter saying that he now had all the money he required and asked her to come back to him. She had not replied to his letter but a day or so later he had spotted her in a cab in Paris and followed her back to her rooms. He then showed her a quantity of jewels and told her these had belonged to the Duchess of Sutherland. She was so fascinated by the sight of such an array of splendours that she readily decided to forget past differences and make up again. Fortunately for Johnson (if not for the Duchess) he had all the jewellery back in his pocket when a French policeman called at the room but the *gendarme* seemed to be satisfied that nothing was amiss and left without taking any further action.

On 22 October Johnson and Mrs Ronald returned separately to London and Johnson began to dispose of some of the items and get others reset or made-up into earrings, pins, studs and rings. In the Brown Bear Public House in Worship Street, Shoreditch, one evening, not only did he consume a large amount of whisky and champagne but changed £500 in gold for the publican's cheque. Such a show of new-found wealth would not long escape the notice of the authorities. Johnson then went to Mrs Morris's house in Cathcart Road to nurse his hangover and hide what little now remained of the jewellery.

So much for the drink. What about the woman?

Mrs Ronald seemed to become over-anxious about her predicament and on the advice of her sister went to Scotland Yard and gave evidence about Johnson's involvement with the robbery. On 31 October Johnson called at her Brighton home but she told him that she thought he was nothing but a thief and wished to have no more to do with him. After a violent row Johnson struck Mrs Ronald. He then returned to London and, as we now know, over-indulged and ended up in the boarding house in Fulham where he was later to be arrested.

The prosecution took some delight in outlining the prisoner's career of crime – he was a well-known and experienced crook who "did not waste his time on small matters". Apart from a theft of a pocket-book from a diamond merchant in a Holborn restaurant and a theft of money in Monte Carlo many of the crimes for which he had been known to the police and had earlier served prison sentences had been committed in railway stations. It was claimed that for some five years he had been under observation by most experienced detectives at railway stations and it was sadly reported "more for his skill than theirs that nothing had come of that observation" (*The Times*, 5 January 1899).

The defence lawyer pointed out that after his quarrel with Mrs Ronald with whom he was infatuated he had "by chance" been in the railway station when the Duchess and her party arrived and sudden temptation and not a preconceived plan had led him to carry out the theft. He had acted alone with no gang of thieves involved. It was stressed that Johnson had never met the Duchess's maid and there had been no involvement by the maid in the theft. He pled guilty to the theft.

On 18 January Johnson was brought up for sentencing. It had been hoped that the postponement of the case would give him the opportunity to give information which might lead to the recovery of the jewels. He had not co-operated and had persistently refused to reveal anything further. Out of the total value of £25,000 or so only £4000-£5000 worth of jewellery had been recovered. It was ordered that £320 which had been found on his possession should be given to the Duchess and Johnson himself was given a seven-year sentence.

Although the jewels were never recovered one expects they would have been well insured and the Duchess did not lose financially out of the Great Jewel Theft. Whatever happened to them may remain a mystery but at least justice was seen to be done and Johnson was incarcerated. The case had been solved. The men at Scotland Yard had triumphed.

One mystery remained, however. Who was the unidentified lady? Why was her identity concealed? One wonders if we had met 'Mrs Ronald' under her real name elsewhere in the story? We may never know!

Sherlock Holmes had been needed after all.

PART FOUR

A View To Sutherland

Heap on more wood! – the wind is chill;
But let it whistle as it will,
We'll keep our Christmas merry still!
SIR WALTER SCOTT – from *Marmion*

CHAPTER SEVENTEEN

The Many Houses Of A Dowager-Duchess

O Woman! in our hours of ease,
Uncertain, coy, and hard to please.
SIR WALTER SCOTT – from *Marmion*

When one has a lot of money there is much temptation to spend it. When one feels that one has been grievously wronged there is perhaps an even greater temptation to spend in order to get even with those who caused you mischief. The Dowager-Duchess in her desire to remain upsides with the Sutherland family desired to have lots of property. Unlike the Sutherlands who had long inherited vast wealth and much property Mary Caroline was relatively new to spectacular wealth and in order to collect properties she had, by and large, to buy them or even build them from scratch.

"Prodigious" is a word loved by Sir Walter Scott. It fairly sums up his vast literary output. It can also with much truth be the adjective applied to the Dowager-Duchess's propensity and ability to acquire property. If there was any truth in the dictum of Oscar Wilde's Lady Bracknell that " three addresses always inspire confidence, even in tradesmen" then the Dowager-Duchess inspired much confidence for she had much property.

She had, of course, inherited Hyde Farm, near Taunton, as well as London property from her first husband and had acquired the Sutherland Manor Estate in Florida and the small Rawlins Estate at Hanford in Staffordshire from the estate of the 3rd Duke but the out-of-court settlement following the will dispute had not only "robbed" her of the Cambusmore Estate (which the Duke had hoped to dis-entail and give to her) but had failed to provide her with Tittensor Chase (which she had leased) or even the shooting lodge at Tongue (which she had built). The settlement of the dispute had, however, given her ample funds to indulge in property acquisition and for the rest of her life that seems to have become a high priority.

Her first steps into property procurement were perhaps a rather inauspicious start for a Dowager-Duchess – she bought an inn. (This is perhaps suggestive of the fact she was a lady with no great taste and discernment but that would be a rather rash assessment.) She had the financial means to indulge herself and the facility of employing very able architects who perhaps gave her what she wanted (she was a very determined lady) but who were able to temper her worst excesses. She actually, and possibly to the surprise of many, therefore acquired and created some very fine homes. Apart from having lots of money, she seems to have had some flair in her choice of buildings and in how to develop them. She has to be given considerable credit in the results even if only to praise her good fortune in her choice of architects and builders who transformed dreams into realities.

Firstly, she acquired property on the south bank of the Thames and near Windsor. Although it was all rather charming in its own way it was a little unbecoming for a Duchess.

The Willows was a rather nice old house but it had a rather chequered career although its once reedy waterbound grounds had now given way to an attractive garden which swept down to the Thames. By the late eighteenth century the house had become a well-known landmark for travellers who were served refreshments under the willow trees on its lawn. More recently it had been the home of Roger Eykyn, one-time Liberal Member of Parliament for Windsor, who sold the property to the Duchess in 1893. Although the setting of the Willows was generally regarded as idyllic the house itself was far from ideal. It had been a fine house but it was not a grand enough house for a Duchess. She, therefore, set about transforming and enlarging the house, indeed she almost entirely demolished the old house in order to make way for the vast sprawling mansion she desired to possess.

The Willows had not been a house of great antiquity or of celebrated architecture. Nearby, however, were two magnificent houses which provided models to be admired and emulated. About two miles up river stands the splendid old half-timbered brick Ockwells Manor which had been in the Norrys family for over 400 years. One of its great glories was the collection of heraldic or armorial glass in the windows of the Great Hall which had been placed there by Sir John Norrys when he built the house in the fifteenth century, for he had been proud of his noble lineage. Across the river sits the manor-house of Dorney Court with its medley of gables and its mellow half-timbered and pinkish brick walls which had been the home of the Palmers since 1620. Both of these supplied examples of families of great pedigree in houses of long tradition – they therefore were houses to be envied as much as admired. These two houses became her reference points for the transformation of the Willows from pleasant but nondescript former inn to a neo-Tudor manor. The Duchess had taken a fancy to Dorney and Ockwells and she got her builder, Mr Charles F. Kearley, to make The Willows into one of the grandest of houses on Thameside and one more befitting her status. She may have only been a Duchess for ten years but hers too was a family of long if not noble lineage.

Kearley had transformed himself from small-time Uxbridge builder and plumber into a Kensington-based, well-known and prosperous tradesman. He considered himself to be "builder and contractor, house and estate agent, interior and general decorator, sanitary engineer &c": he was obviously a good man to know.

In 1898 she purchased the adjacent property of Surly Hall but in spite of its high-sounding name it was more of a public house than a country house. It was a frequent and favourite haunt of Eton students and other boating people for it had its own moorings.

By the late summer of 1901 the Duchess had decided that being landlady of an inn was not quite commensurate with being a lady with land and that she would not seek to renew its licence. She wrote to the local licensing sessions declaring that

> the needs of the neighbourhood are amply supplied by other licensed premises . . . it seems to me that it is unnecessary and inexpedient to keep the house open. By this means there will be a slight reduction in the number of public houses (*The Times*, 21 September 1901,7).

It was one of the Duchess's rare public-spirited acts but there was an ulterior motive. Always the great schemer, she had new ideas and she planned to demolish poor old Surly Hall and build another house more to her taste. Surly Hall therefore lost its licence, was closed down, pulled down, and in its place was built a new black and white pile to be known (perhaps not surprisingly) as Sutherland Grange.

The Duchess also desired a fine London house. If ever a house was suitable for Mary Caroline, Dowager-Duchess of Sutherland, it really had to be 45 Belgrave Square. It had been, until her death in 1894, the town-house of another aristocratic old lady – Caroline, Duchess of Montrose. Although the Duke of Montrose had died in 1874 and his widow subsequently remarried twice, becoming in effect Mrs Stirling-Crawford and Mrs Milner she still retained the lofty title of Dowager-Duchess of Montrose. Perhaps Duchess Blair looked and learned from that old Dowager. Our Duchess moved in during 1895 and it became the principal matrimonial home during her marriage to Sir Albert Rollit.

Though she was to ever retain a pied-à-terre in central London, in order to have a more commodious London house where she and her husband could entertain in some style, 'The Cottage', at Kingsbury, was built in 1899. To call it a cottage was a misnomer – a piece of inverted snobbery – for it was a most attractive villa and indeed was later to be called 'Kingsbury Manor' – a name perhaps more suited to its size and pretensions. It was a charming house set in an attractive garden. Of mock Elizabethan design it had spacious public rooms at ground level and equally spacious bedrooms above.

The house was designed by William West Neve, the first apprentice and later assistant of the highly regarded Richard Norman Shaw. Its size lent itself to institutional use and it is now a residential home and its grounds serve as a public park. The coach-house and stables were later to achieve considerable fame for it was from there that John Logie Baird conducted early experiments in television transmittance.

Her marriage to Sir Albert was perhaps doomed to failure. T.P O'Conner of the *Daily Telegraph* believed it to be a "daring matrimonial enterprise" and considered that "anybody who knew anything of the two middle-aged lovers might have foretold the result" (*Surrey Advertiser*, 19 August 1922). They agreed to separate in 1904 and even publicly intimated the fact. Sir Albert went to live in the large rambling house of St Anne's Hill, Chertsey.

However, we must return to the Duchess.

As she was beginning to get on in years and therefore perhaps in increasingly indifferent health and with two little granddaughters the sea-breeze and the beaches of Hove possibly made it an ideal choice. In 1908 therefore she purchased a house on the edge of the esplanade – it had a superb seafront location if it did not have any great architectural qualities. Designed by a London architect, Herbert Bignold, the house was designed to be the first of a stretch of terrace houses and was known as 'Swancoe' but the Dowager-Duchess changed its name to 'Casa Amoena' – a name derived from the Latin meaning pleasant or delightful. Casa Amoena was to end its days as a café and one can imagine the Duchess would not have been amused if she had been able to foretell what the future promised for her holiday home. A café indeed!

From her comfortable home in stately 45 Belgrave Square the Dowager-Duchess of Sutherland, in the early years of the century, possessed a property portfolio of impressive proportions. She owned a fine house at Windsor with its recently constructed ancillary house – Sutherland Grange, a 'cottage' at Kingsbury, a holiday house at Hove, an estate in Florida and land in Somerset and Staffordshire with maybe even a few lesser bits into the bargain. It was a collection most people would have been proud of and one that most people would have been satisfied with. A different house for each day of the week must surely be considered ample. The Duchess, however, did not – she still yearned for a particular house. She missed the grandeur of Dunrobin, Lilleshall, Trentham and Stafford House. She lacked a truly ducal seat.

CHAPTER EIGHTEEN

From Culrain To Carbisdale

My castles are my King's alone,
From turret to foundation-stone.
SIR WALTER SCOTT – from *Marmion*

Although she had acquired many properties – in the sunshine of Florida, on the seafront near Brighton, in the centre of London, on the banks of the Thames at Windsor, and even a farm with one hundred and nine acres in Somerset – the Duchess remained dissatisfied. She had been thwarted in her attempts to gain a great country house and to have an estate of vast acres.

For a time the Duchess's family leased Inveran Lodge in remote, rugged and magnificent Wester Ross. Inveran faced south and overlooked the River Ewe, barely a few metres from the north-west tip of delightful Loch Maree where the River Ewe has its source and only a little distance from the mouth of the rushing River Inveran. Part of the Mackenzie of Gairloch's estates, Inveran had been the occasional boyhood home of Osgood Mackenzie, celebrated as the creator of the splendid sub-tropical gardens of Inverewe, just a few miles to the west. Sadly, Inveran suffered the same fate as Inverewe House – the latter was burnt down in 1914 (and a new house built on the site in 1937) whereas Inveran Lodge was destroyed by fire in 1968 and has been replaced by a modern bungalow.

Loch Maree had been another spot visited by Queen Victoria – a boulder in front of Loch Maree Hotel records her visit of 1877 when she stayed in a "nice little house". The

Gaelic inscription tells that she "in her kindness, agreed that this stone should be a memorial of the pleasure she experienced in coming to this quarter of Ross" (Polson, 1908, 44). The Victoria Falls nearby were so named in her honour.

In the late nineteenth century Inveran had been the home of John Dixon, an Englishman who loved the West Highlands and its people and wrote what has proved to be the definitive book on the area. Its title certainly revealed its all-embracing remit, suggesting that few stones would be left unturned – *Gairloch in North West Ross-shire, its records, traditions, inhabitants and natural beauty with a Guide to Gairloch and Loch Maree.* A title which perhaps gives more of a mouthful than simply a taste of the area or of the full contents of the book. Although first published in 1886 it remains, as the totality of its scope given in its title might suggest, *the* indispensable guide to the district.

The distinguished wildlife artist, Archibald Thorburn, and his wife spent a very long honeymoon at Inveran and he executed some charming watercolour sketches of the surrounding countryside while there. Thorburn was considered the most outstanding illustrator of animals and birds and his paintings now fetch considerable sums. His book on British Birds of 1916 is itself a collectors' item.

While Thorburn captured the flora and fauna in ink and watercolour a later owner of Inveran used gun and rod for his pursuits. He was the noted High Court Judge, Lord Mackenzie, and had listed his recreations as being hunting, shooting and fishing. One can well imagine that a finer spot than Inveran would be difficult to find for those who indulge in any such country, sporting, pursuits. The one aspect of the natural history which can be considered a veritable drawback is that curse of the West Highlands – the midge. One visitor to Loch Maree summed it up in verse –

> I love her silver birken trees,
> But I detest the midges (Polson, 1908, 44).

It might not be very great poetry but the sentiments were no doubt real and one can almost feel the midge bites.

Leasing part of someone else's Highland estates is not the same thing as owning an estate oneself. Duchess Blair did not have a Scottish seat of her own and yet she would be well aware that others with little or no Highland connection had built or were building mighty houses for themselves. The late Victorian/Edwardian age was one when some of the wealthiest of the English and Lowland Scottish nouveau riche took to acquiring Highland estates and demanded appropriately grand shooting lodges or even suitably baronial castles from which to lord it over their vast acres.

Many of these 'incomers' had used old Alexander Ross of Inverness, the doyen of Highland architects, to design their Highland seat (C. W. Dyson Perrins – of Worcester sauce's Lea & Perrins – at Ardross Castle, for example) but others employed architects from the South. The splendidly picturesque red sandstone Glenborrodale Castle, in remote Ardnamurchan, was built for Charles Dunnell Rudd, one of the 'Randlords' and friend and associate of Cecil Rhodes, who had made a fortune out of South African diamond mining. Glenborrodale was completed in 1902 and built to designs by Sydney Mitchell of Edinburgh. Sir George Bullough, the Accrington textile magnate, built, at a cost reputed to be in the region of £250,000, the vast red sandstone mock-castellated extravaganza which is Kinloch Castle, Rum. It was completed in 1901 and designed by Messrs Leeming and Leeming of London and Halifax. James Macvicar Anderson, originally from Edinburgh but London-based, provided the final drawings for splendid Inverlochy Castle, near Fort William, which was completed in 1892 as the seat of Lord Abinger. Anderson had earlier produced the final touches for Glengarry Castle, in the Great Glen, which his uncle, the great Victorian country-house architect, David Bryce, had begun for Edward Ellice MP.

Sir Sisismund Neumann, a financier of German Jewish stock and another South African randlord, had turned himself into a landlord in the Highlands with the estate of Glenmuick on Deeside and with it acquired the nickname "MacNeumann".

Previously he had leased Invercauld Castle which had earlier been suitably baronialised for its Scottish owner (Miss Farquarson) by London architect J. T. Wimperis in the 1870's. Mark Girouard has delightfully suggested that "to employ him was rather like ordering a house from Harrods" (Girouard, 1979, 431). Glenmuick had been built in 1872 by the great railway builder and financier Sir Morton Peto and its seventy-five feet tower and pink granite Tudor walls made it a notable landmark. The Prince of Wales, later King Edward VII, was to become a regular visitor to Glenmuick and to Tulchan Lodge at Advie on Speyside where another financier Arthur Sassoon had his shooting lodge. George Coats (of Messrs J. & P. Coats the thread-makers) was to acquire the former Cunliffe Brooks estate of the Forest of Glen Tanar, another old haunt of the Prince's. The delightfully named Mrs Umfreville Pickering had got the London firm of Niven and Wigglesworth to design her magnificent baronial edifice of Kincardine House on Deeside. Sir Weetman Pearson (later Lord Cowdray) became the tenant of the vast estate of Dunecht, formerly the Earl of Crawford's Aberdeenshire seat, and he was later to purchase this estate outright. There seemed to be no end to 'outsiders' acquiring extensive hold-ings in the Highlands. Duchess Blair was doubtless green with envy as she scanned the gossip columns and listened avidly to every piece of property-buying tittle tattle.

One of the seats of the former owner of her Belgrave Square house, the Dowager-Duchess of Montrose, had been Buchanan Castle near Loch Lomond – a splendid baronial pile designed by William Burn, the London-based Scot who became one of the leading country-house architects of the mid-nineteenth century. A new Buchanan Castle had become necessary because the old one had burnt down during one of Caroline's frequent stays in London. Carelessness on the part of a drunken housekeeper was deemed responsible. The story almost transports us back to the fire at Dunrobin when too many 'cups of comfort' were also blamed and when the earlier Duchess-Countess had been also frequently absent.

Duchess Blair perhaps considered that the old Duchess of Montrose had at least got a new castle: this Duchess had never had a replacement for Dunrobin.

Some of her neighbours in Belgrave Square had also acquired Highland estates. Sir John Stirling Maxwell of Pollok, at No 48, had Corrour at Loch Ossian, Inverness-shire, where he had recently erected a shooting lodge while the ship-owner, Sir Charles Cayzer, at No 34 (later he moved to No 27), not content with estates at Ralston, near Paisley, and Gartmore, near Aberfoyle, had also acquired an estate in Angus on which he was to build his own castle – Kinpurnie. He was also later to acquire the great baronial splendours of Ballikinrain Castle, near Balfron, in Stirlingshire. It was regarded as David Bryce's grandest essay in the Scots Baronial style. The Duke of Richmond and Gordon and the Earl of March (both at No 49) already had substantial northern property. One can imagine the jealousy welling up at No 45.

Even the Duchess Blair's cabinet-maker Walter Shoolbred, of the London firm James Shoolbred and Co, had a mock Tudor shooting-lodge built overlooking Loch Glass in Easter Ross. Shoolbreds of Tottenham Court Road were a pioneering department store and although commencing as drapers had in 1873 blossomed into cabinet-making and upholstery and were later to be swallowed up by neighbouring Maples, another of the great firms with which the Duchess did business. Not only would they have made her Holloway cell into a pleasant chamber but they would most likely have added nice furnishings to all her houses as well as to all others embarking on the creating of country house homes.

Everybody, it must have seemed, was getting a Highland estate with magnificent shooting lodge if not a Scottish Castle; everybody that is, with one notable exception – the one particular Duchess of Sutherland who ought to have had one.

It was a situation which had long troubled the Dowager-Duchess and it was something she proposed to remedy.

Since the Sutherland family had compelled her to yield her

toehold at Tongue Lodge, scuppered her chances of having Cambusmore and finally forced her out of Dunrobin, having no intention of allowing her ever again to have a foothold in their county. Duchess Blair would therefore require to be content with property outwith Sutherland. It may not have been a greatly upsetting dilemma for she had ample funds to have a house built to her design and specification and Scotland is full of fine picturesque, if not economically sound, estates. One can imagine she would not have settled for anything but the best and she had money galore to indulge herself. The Dowager-Duchess of Sutherland desired a great house and would get one. It was to be as simple as that. Getting a suitable property on which to erect a fine home became the one obsessive goal.

In the latter days of the nineteenth century a new magazine appeared which did much to arouse an interest in architecture and in fine houses. For those in 'the search for style' *Country Life* would be a welcome friend. It also carried an abundance of advertisements for fine houses and country estates. In 1904 it had an article on old Ockwells Hall, just a few miles from the Willows, and that might have rekindled her wish to have a great hall with heraldic glass to display her nobility.

In the early years of the twentieth century however a most suitable, almost irresistible, property came on the market and Duchess Blair unhesitatingly snapped it up.

Built in the early 1870s Culrain Lodge was an elegant enough but rather unpretentious two-storey mid-Victorian mansionhouse with white cement-rendered walls and its roof a medley of gables and slated conical towers. Although a shooting lodge it was more akin to a large suburban villa than a great country house. The lodge was about half a mile from the village of Culrain (which means 'mossy place'), about four miles from Ardgay on the southern bank of the Kyle and up river and over the bridge from the Sutherland village of Bonar Bridge.

The house was set on the hillside amid pleasantly wooded policies and not far off was the little railway station of

Culrain, at the southern end of the mighty Invershin Railway Viaduct which carries the Highland Railway northwards to Sutherland and the far North. Culrain Lodge was therefore a most conveniently accessible property. The Culrain Estate had belonged to James Simpson JP who farmed its rough acres and had served as Sheriff Substitute for Lochaber at Fort William from 1873 until his retiral in 1894. On his death, in 1898, his wife, Jane McKenzie, continued to administer the estate for a few more years until it was subsequently sold, in 1903, to Mary Caroline, Duchess of Sutherland, and her husband, Sir Albert Rollit. When they separated in 1904 the Duchess assumed entire ownership and Sir Albert leased the estate of Manar, near Inverurie, in Aberdeenshire.

No doubt Culrain Lodge had not been bought for its architectural merit, in so far as it had little, but it had been bought for its superb location. It stood on the very northern edge of Ross-shire and overlooked the Kyle of Sutherland. From its windows one looked across to Sutherland. It offered the perfect prospect of Sutherland. Everything and everyone going to Sutherland by road or rail had to pass Culrain.

The great eighteenth-century landscape gardener, Launcelot Brown, who had carried out extensive works at Trentham, earned his soubriquet "Capability" because he informed his potential clients that their estates offered great capabilities for improvement. In a later age the Culrain estate, too, offered many capabilities. Culrain Lodge was not of palatial proportions nor did it have the ducal qualities demanded by a Dowager-Duchess but the estate did indeed offer very real possibilities. A fabulously rich Duchess might transform it and make long cherished dreams come true.

The location of Culrain Lodge may have appealed for it is just across the Kyle from the estate of Balblair and is also just south of another Inveran – this time a small private estate in Sutherland, But Culrain Lodge may also have been a place of very special affection for the Duchess for it seems that it had been a favourite rendezvous spot for her and the 3rd Duke. For a lady as romantic as the Duchess, the site of Culrain could not be surpassed. For a lady rumoured to be as spiteful as the Duchess it equally could not be bettered.

It is also a little ironic that she should have purchased Culrain, on the last frontier of Ross-shire and yet just over the boundary in Sutherland, just across the Kyle, there is that estate named Inveran. Her holiday home of Inveran, in the wilds of Wester Ross, had therefore shared a common name with part of her beloved Sutherland and was within a stone's throw of her newly-acquired Culrain. Indeed, is seems as if someone who did not know their geography might just have leased the wrong one in 1900 and had meant to lease a piece of Sutherland and not a Lodge on Loch Maree-side.

Having acquired the unprepossessing Culrain Lodge consideration had now to be given as to how to create there her very own fairy tale. She had vivid recollections of her happy years at Dunrobin and had a wealth of experience gained from her building exploits south of the border but building a new stately home was a new experience.

If she did not visit herself she would certainly have heard about Skibo Castle. She would no doubt at least have seen it from afar as it was taking shape on the north bank of the Dornoch Firth some twelve miles or so to the east.

Skibo had been purchased by Andrew Carnegie in 1898 and he had begun to enlarge and remodel the castle which had only been rebuilt as recently as 1880. By 1903 Skibo had become one of the grandest Baronial edifices in Scotland – regarded as "a 'royal palace' outshining Balmoral" (Read, 1972, 46). Carnegie had become the richest man in the world when he sold out his huge steel-making interests and had decided to become a greater philanthropist than he had been a capitalist. Proud of his Scottish origins he desired a suitably ostentatious house to be his Scottish home where he could entertain and where his young daughter could share in that heritage. He reputedly spent £100,000 on making Skibo into the home he wanted.

Duchess Blair would have heard of, even if she had not seen, its great five light windows to the staircase depicting scenes of Carnegie's life and family history. It would no doubt remind her of windows which she had long admired at Ockwells Manor at Bray where she had been mightily impressed by the heraldic glass placed there by the Norrys family many centuries ago. She perhaps thought that her castle should also have stained glass depicting her family's dynastic history – had she not become the Duchess of Sutherland, albeit that it was now simply an honorary title.

Duchess May would also be well aware of the great fairy-tale-like French château being created near Avoch (pronounced Auch as in loch) for a Director and one-time Chairman of the Highland Railway and former Ceylonese tea and rubber plantation owner, James Douglas Fletcher. He had succeeded to his father's estates in 1885 and was regarded as "one of the most progressive and enlightened of the younger landlords of the North" (*Builder*, 9 September 1893). Rosehaugh was to become a truly magnificent pile and although Alexander Ross had carried out work there in the past for James Fletcher, his son had turned to William Flockhart for its massive and sumptuous redevelopment. Messrs Foster and Dicksee of Rugby had been entrusted with the building contract. It was to have bedrooms in Jacobean, Georgian, Elizabethan and William & Mary styles (*Building News*, 11 December 1903) with magnificent plasterwork and it had such a collection of antique chimney pieces (one of which had come from King James I & VI's palace in Kent) and doorways, tapestries and works of art that contemporary comment stated "the interior is so full of works of art that it. . . is almost a museum of antiquities" (*Building News*, I January 1904). The Duchess may have visited Rosehaugh; she would certainly hear of it. Lessons were to be learned.

She would also no doubt hear how old James Fletcher, who had first acquired Rosehaugh in 1864 and built the earlier mansion, when having a tower added to his house of Letham Grange, in Angus, was very exacting in his demands and if it was not to his liking simply told his builders to "Tak it doon". The tower was taken down and rebuilt several times. The

Duchess, one can well imagine, would not be willing to accept anything but the best of quality and good craftsmanship either. She too wanted nothing but the best. If others could have showplaces so would she.

Carbisdale had a grander ring to it than Culrain. It was also a more historic name for Montrose's last great battle had become known as the Battle of Carbisdale but thereby hangs a tale and it is a tale that must wait until the next chapter. Acquiring a battlefield somehow seems entirely appropriate – the Dowager-Duchess had had to wage war to obtain the funding for her castle.

The castle has had a bad press – thought of as ugly and grotesque – and we have been encouraged to believe that although the Duchess may have had an abundance of money she had a shortage of taste. This view is largely unfair and unfounded. Carbisdale is very much a product of its time: it may be a monumentally pretentious pile of Edwardian kitsch but it is also a Baronial tower-cum-modern palace of much dignity and not a little beauty. Its simulated antiquity gives it a presence and it is hard to imagine any design treatment which would have been more appropriate or would have looked finer on its magnificent location.

When Culrain came on the market, we were told she "instructed an Inverness architect to travel north and survey it" (MacGregor, 1965, 60) and establish if she could have the building she wished on the site. It has been assumed that John Robertson who had designed St Anne's Church in Strathpeffer had carried out the site inspection and the design work. If he did (and the writer remains sceptical on the issue) then in many ways he was an ideal choice – if he was considered good enough by her hateful step-children to design their mother's memorial then he must be good enough for her.

The very affluent John Drewe, co-founder of Home & Colonial Stores, had instructed his architect Edwin Lutyens that he wished to build his Castle Drogo at a cost not exceeding £50,000 and that a further £10,000 could be spent on the garden. Lutyens was unsure of what these sums meant in real constructional terms and had written to his wife in August 1910 –

> I suppose £60,000 sounds a lot to you but I don't know what it means. If I look at Westminster Abbey it is an absurd – trivial amount. If I look at a dear little old world two-roomed cottage it merely looks a vast unmanageable amount (Percy and Ridley, 1985, 199).

It is worthwhile putting such a sum in perspective. Such a sum would in fact have been sufficient "for three hundred or more Labourer's cottages" (Powell, 1980, 51).

It is unlikely that Duchess Blair instructed her architect as Drewe had done. She simply seems to have desired a great house and had sufficient funds to get what she wanted. Drewe had to cut back on his grand design – not so the Duchess. Whether she fell out with Robertson or just felt he was out of touch with her wishes we do not know. The job might just have been beyond Robertson for he was a prolific architect of Highland churches but had little experience of stately-home building. With the departure of her Scottish architect she then did as others had done and got the well-known English practice of Weatherley & Jones in to finish the project.

Quite why W. S. Weatherley and F. E. Jones were appointed also remains a bit of a mystery. That they were appointed is beyond dispute. They too were church architects and Weatherley especially carried out superb pieces of church building as well as some sensitive restoration work. Both had trained in the office of that great Gothic Revivalist, Sir George Gilbert Scott. Weatherley had remained there while Jones went as assistant to Scott's son, John Oldrid Scott before they joined together in partnership. Their church work would probably be known to Duchess Blair's brother, Rev. Arthur Michell; indeed he had been curate at St Mary's Upton-cum-Chalvey when John Oldrid Scott had carried out extensive work and would doubtless have met Jones at that time. A Yorkshireman like Sir Albert Rollit would also be well acquainted with Weatherley and Jones' work for they had designed in London the Yorkshire Society's School and had carried out work in Yorkshire at Thorpe Hall for the Macdonald of the Isles. Weatherley and Jones had also designed some castles and houses in Holland for Dutch aristocrats as well as being architects for a wide and varied range of work. Other projects included the popular Hatchetts Hotel and White Horse Cellars in Piccadilly.

Maybe one of the reasons for their appointment by Duchess Blair was that Weatherley and Jones had also carried out work in Windsor for one of the Leveson-Gowers and one of her stepsons, the Earl of Cromarty, was married to the daughter of Lord Macdonald. Internal wrangles within the Macdonald family had caused deep division and separated the 'of the Isles' branch from the historic clan lands. To further fuel an old quarrel might not have been the Dowager-Duchess's aim, perhaps she had simply employed them at the Willows, found them to be entirely satisfactory and thus used them again in the Highlands. Carbisdale is certainly as much an English manorial house as a Scottish Baronial castle.

Work began on the excavations for Carbisdale's foundations in 1907. Alasdair Alpin Macgregor tells that "in the presence of a large and representative gathering, the foundation stone . . . was laid in 1910" (Macgregor, 1965, 58) but as the castle had first made an appearance on the Valuation Roll for 1909-10 it must have been built in sufficient form for the Duchess to have taken up residence by that date. It seems likely that she resided "in one wing while workmen built and hammered in the others" (*Scottish Field*, January 1945).

Messrs D. & J. Milligan of Ayr were the builders of Carbisdale. They had carried out many major building contracts including some of the grandest of Victorian houses and had a reputation as good craftsmen. They had built Andrew Carnegie's Skibo as well as Logan House in Galloway, Glenapp Castle, Ayrshire, CastleToward in Cowal, Inverlochy Castle near Fort William, Inveree House in Wester Ross, and the Stathpeffer Hotel in Easter Ross. In 1907 they were also finishing to the neo-baronialised Dunbeath Castle in Caithness.

According to Macgregor Carbisdale Castle "took £68,000 to build and £100,000 to furnish (Macgregor, 1965, 59). This figure suggests that while the Duchess built lavishly and well she did not simply splash money around. Maybe the Sutherlands, if they were the paymasters, had imposed a ceiling on the expenditure! Maybe she was simply well satisfied with what she was getting and did not need to spend more!

The Castle gained the name of Spite Castle, for its very location and siting made it scorn on Sutherland. According to Macgregor, in building it she had renewed "her former vindictiveness" (Macgregor, 1965, 66). The Sutherlands, on their journeys to and from the South, could not fail to see it being built stone by stone as it reared up from Carbisdale Heights and every time they saw it they would be reminded of Duchess Blair and old animosities would be rekindled. The Sutherlands, as they steamed past in their private train, reputedly used to pull down the blinds of their carriage as Carbisdale came into view so that they did not have to see it. Perhaps they simply cringed in embarrassed silence at the prospect of seeing this monster they had, if not funded, at least been instrumental in creating by their own entrenched attitudes. "If only things had been different," they perhaps mused quietly to themselves as once again a sly look was taken before the blinds were drawn. They might have detested her and her castle but they would wish to know what was happening even if they might pretend otherwise.

The ill-feeling was certainly not confined to the 4th Duke and Duchess of Sutherland: Duchess Blair retained a simmering resentment. The dominant feature of the castle is its great tower with a clock on three of its faces. There was no clock put on the wall facing Sutherland. She herself is reported to have said "She would not even give them the time of day". Spite was indeed a key ingredient in its conception as well as its execution.

Supposedly designed in different architectural styles to

reflect different periods it therefore suggested that it was an old building with a long history and had gained additions with the passage of time. Some differences may also reflect different architects and their work. The truth of the matter is that we know very little about the constructional history of Carbisdale Castle. It is almost a greater enigma than its owner. It may not be an impregnable castle but it has an unfathomable story.

Built of grey rubble stonework with polished sandstone dressings it is basically a two-storey plus attic building but the nature of its site has dictated that it has two additional service floors below the principal entrance floor. This adds to its stature as viewed from afar and gives it a much grander aspect. A terrace sweeps round its southern face from which three great canted bay windows soar skywards. Its roofline is a mixture of fancy carved gabled dormers, crenellated battlements, corbelled turrets and Dutch gables. One approaches it across a wide entrance court where a mighty stone *porte-cochère* shelters the entrance door and gives it a stately status. From near and far it is a building of presence.

It is also a building full of rich and quirky detailing – cute little finials crown its dormers and winged figures decorate the rainheads. Nevertheless, it is a building where 'big' has to be the overworked adjective – everything about Carbisdale is larger than life. It has reputedly over 200 rooms and it seems to have more windows than anywhere else. It is supposed to have one window more than Dunrobin (that figures, doesn't it?) and its lofty situation means that it dominates the scene like few other buildings. Castle Drogo might dominate its Devon and Dartmoor landscape but the scale is smaller. Dunrobin is only truly majestic when viewed from its own landscaped terraced gardens or from the shoreline but Carbisdale commands our attention from afar. Without Carbisdale the Kyle of Sutherland would simply be a pleasant but unspectacular piece of Highland scenery – with Carbisdale Castle it is truly magnificent.

Old Culrain Lodge, having served its purpose as a temporary home until Carbisdale began to rise on its site, was demolished. Rumour long persisted that it was incorporated into another building but this was not so – Duchess Blair might have been sad for nostalgic, romantic reasons to see it disappear but with an eye to present needs and status it was expendable. In its place a new Tudoresque service complex of stables and coachouse known as Carbisdale Court was erected. A wide Tudor arch gives access to the battlemented two-storey square courtyard. It is simply a less grand but equally solid place of mock-castellated building.

The castellated gate piers at the roadside forming the entrance to the drive give a foretaste of the neo-baronial might of Carbisdale Castle at the top of the drive. They are the trumpets at the distant gate of the last and possibly the most romantic of Scottish castles. It owed its very being to the fact that she had loved and married the 3rd Duke of Sutherland. She may also have loved Sutherland but she loathed and detested the Sutherlands.

The telegraphic code for its builders D. & J. Milligan had been 'Monument" – one can scarce think of a more fitting description to describe one of their greatest works, Carbisdale Castle.

CHAPTER NINETEEN

An Historical Interlude –
The Battle Lost

Soldier, rest! thy warfare o'er,
Sleep the sleep that knows not breaking,
Dream of battled fields no more,
Days of danger, nights of waking.
SIR WALTER SCOTT – from *The Lady of the Lake*

One of the greatest of all Scottish military heroes (or villains, depending on one's viewpoint) was the legendary Marquis of Montrose. At his birth his father was reported as stating that "he would trouble all Scotland" (Williams, n.d., 5) – it was almost prophetic for he was indeed to cause much trouble. He was without doubt the most colourful and romantic of all seventeenth-century figures and in all Scottish history he has scarce an equal. He is also one whose name will ever be associated with Carbisdale. In a sense it was he who put it on the map.

The seventeenth century may have been a more religious age than our own but it was also one of greater fanaticism. The seventeenth century was therefore one of conflict – a United Kingdom of 1603 had not led to a united kingdom. The regal reality was not manifest throughout the land. Faction and faith had got in the way of peaceful co-existence and the death of a very shrewd ruler like James VI and I had robbed the kingdom of the unifying force at the centre. Charles I came to the throne in 1625 but his intense convictions and headstrong opinions invariably seemed more like interference and intolerance. They did not pass muster with those who regarded Christ as the true King and who held little respect for the Divine Right of earthly kings. The Protestant Reformer, Andrew Melville, had declared the doctrine of the 'Twa Kingdoms' by which there was a kingdom which was the realm of the monarch and the Kingdom of Christ in which the earthly king was but God's 'silly Vassal'. In an age when politics and religion were so interlocked the things that were God's were not however very easily differentiated from the things that were Caesar's.

In August 1633 William Laud was promoted to Archbishop of Canterbury and he strenuously endeavoured to bring the Kirk in Scotland into line with the Anglican Church. Simmering resentment came to a head with the introduction of a new prayer book. The National Covenant was drawn up to defend the religious and constitutional liberties of the Scottish nation. Charles regarded it as an act of open rebellion rather than simply a protest and therefore decided that force would be required to bring his recalcitrant realm to heel.

The Covenanters decided they would meet the threat and resist with force and so raised an army under the seasoned campaigner, General Leslie. Inflexibility and high-handed ecclesiastical policies had caused Covenanters to rise up against their king. The Covenanters firmly believed that they were not only right but that God was on their side. James Graham, Earl of Montrose, had been one of the four noblemen who had drawn up the National Covenant and in 1639, at the head of an army, occupied the city of Aberdeen for the Covenanters. The Treaty of Berwick brought peace between the warring factions and saved Aberdeen from destruction at the hands of the occupying force.

Whether growing disillusionment with Covenanting demands or a perceived easing of the King's position weaned Montrose away from the Covenanters one cannot now say but he moved from a position of hostility to one of amity. Before long he had wholeheartedly embraced the King's cause and like any true convert was most zealous in furthering the adopted aims. In 1644 he became the King's Lieutenant in Scotland and was, all but in name, the commander of the King's forces in Scotland. When the conflict was renewed Montrose was firmly for the King not only as General but as newly elevated Marquis of Montrose. He was now to display his great skill as military leader. Victory followed victory. At Tippermuir the Covenanters were sorely beaten, Aberdeen was retaken for the Crown, the city of Dundee fell to the Royalists, and there were victories at Auldearn, at Alford and the greatest of all at Kilsyth. With this last of his six great victories all Scotland seemed to be within his grasp and the Covenanting force could seemingly do nothing right. Little wonder Montrose was considered "the greatest soldier of his age" (Buchan, 1928, 389).

That no general is greater than the men under his command might be a feature much overlooked by those of the 'History of Great Men' school but it is no less true. Montrose, like any general, proved no better than the force at his disposal. It is a lesson in historiography which can be simply demonstrated. After their succession of victories Montrose's Highland army returned to their glens and without their awesome presence Montrose tasted defeat. At Philiphaugh, at the hands of a reinvigorated Covenanting Army under General Leslie, Montrose's cycle of success came to an abrupt halt. Montrose was not invincible. Forced to leave the field he fled to Norway to ensure that he would live to fight another day.

For the Covenanters, victory at Philiphaugh had surely demonstrated that although God "might justly quarrel with a sinful Nation for their transgression," he also 'powreth out his wrath on their enemies' (Heath, 1650). It had been thus, in their view, as much God's victory as theirs. The idea that God was on their side had given Covenanters renewed strength and they would be ready to fight fearlessly if and when the conflict was rekindled.

With the execution of Charles I, Montrose vowed that he would "dedicate the remainder of my life to avenging the death of the royal martyr, and re-establishing his son upon the throne" (Macgregor, 1939, 224). In fulfilling that promise he returned to his homeland on his mission to retake Scotland. He first landed in Orkney and then crossing the Pentland Firth he arrived on the mainland near Duncansby Head. The march south began and although he seized Dunbeath Castle in Caithness he failed to take Dunrobin Castle – it was perhaps a bad omen. On the evening of 25 April, having crossed the River Oykell, he and his men arrived near Invercharron and supposedly at Carbisdale Loch (Loch a choire), on the slopes of Creag Choineachan, encamped with the Culrain Burn on one flank and the Kyle of Sutherland to the other. The great Marquis, at the head of some 1200 Cavaliers, German or Danish mercenaries and undrilled Orcadians, simply waited. Quite why Montrose waited there will never be known – he may have thought reinforcements would soon arrive or he may have thought any opposition, should it come, would be easily dismissed, giving him time to gather strength. He did not realise that the Covenanters were on the ascendancy and a small force under Lieut. Colonel Strachan had been speedily despatched northwards from Inverness to meet them.

On Saturday 27 April the Covenanters had arrived at Wester Fearn, near Kincardine. The problem for them, as Sunday was fast approaching, was whether to fight that afternoon or delay until Monday for they wished to "decline the hazzard of engaging in the Lords day" (Heath, 1650). Strachan sent a single troop of horse forward and as Montrose's reconnoitering party seemed to have only seen that small force, they reported back accordingly. Montrose probably felt that these horsemen could be easily beaten and therefore he would come down from the hill of Creag Choineachan to deal with these Covenanters and then re-commence his march south.

Whether his information had been at fault or whether he underestimated the size of the opposition will be long debated. The fact remains that Montrose had been unwisely tempted down from his commanding position to the plain. At 3 o'clock in the afternoon Strachan moved towards the enemy. The numerically superior Royalist force offered little resistance and was easily routed by a force of perhaps 230 horsemen and 170 foot. According to Heath's rather none too impartial account –

> "at the first charge made them all to runne: the Lord did strike such a terror into their hearts, as their most resolute Commanders had not the courage to lift up a hand to defend themselves, and our forces without opposition, did execution upon them five or six miles, even till Sunset"(Heath, 1650).

In the Battle of Invercharron of 27 April 1650 some 440 of Montrose's men were taken captive and over 400 slain. Others drowned while trying to escape across the Kyle. It is thought as few as one hundred Royalists escaped to freedom. It was the great general's last battle. It had not been a great battle.

Montrose's own horse was shot from under him and to make his escape he had to discard his sword belt and his easily identifiable coat complete with its Star of St George. On a borrowed horse and wounded he managed to swim across the Kyle and fled up Strath Oykell to the wilds of Assynt.

A shot fired at Col. Strachan struck his belt but he was unharmed. One trooper, who had pursued some of the enemy trying to escape in a small boat, was himself drowned and two others were wounded but these were apparently the only casualties. It is perhaps little wonder that the Covenanters were elated and Heath hastened into print to give his one-sided "true relation of the late great and happy victory obtained by the blessing of God against that Excommunicate and bloody Traytors, James Graham and his Complices, who had invaded this Kingdom" (Heath, 1650). Sir George Douglas was later to suggest the very title of the pamphlet was "a fair specimen of the peculiar tone of unction which characterises its pages" (*Glasgow Herald*, 14 April 1923).

Those who participated in the rout were later rewarded. Heath has told that as regards Strachan "they have given him £1000 English, and a Gold chain: and Hacket 1000 marks

English and Kiffin £50 and to the party that engaged in the service three months pay". (Heath, 1650). The Scottish Committee of Estates had been badly shaken by the news of Montrose's landing in Scotland – they were now obviously delighted at the outcome. It may not have been much of a battle but it had been decisive.

It had been a battle which ended a war.

After two days wandering Montrose stumbled across a small cottage where he was given food and shelter. He was then taken to the home of Neil Macleod, the laird of Assynt. Whether Macleod sought him out or whether Montrose was taken by force or at his own request to Ardvreck Castle we cannot now tell. It seems however that having been initially hospitably entertained Montrose and his companion were handed over to Major General Holbourn at the head of a search party of Covenanting horse. Macleod seems to have earned himself a bounty of some £25,000 Scots and much opprobrium while from Ardvreck Montrose embarked on his last journey. Montrose might have preferred to have met his death in battle for he no doubt realised that "the last blow had been struck, only death awaited" (Buchan, 1928, 361) but he was now at the mercy of others.

'Betrayal' is the strong word which has been used to describe the incident but it may be simply that Macleod had only done what he perceived to be his duty and that had he continued to fraternise with the enemy that might have been regarded as a larger betrayal. It was a time of little trust when passions ran high and the power of the sword was a strong deterrent to charitable action. The Covenanters certainly regarded Montrose as a traitor having formerly been their ally and perhaps 'betrayal' is a two-edged weapon.

Writing around the time of the tercentenary of the battle R. T. Clark suggested defeat at Carbisdale had been "the result of a subordinate's error" (*Glasgow Herald*, 20 May 1950) but generals must surely, in the final analysis, be responsible for all actions. A recent military historian had perhaps wisely concluded that Montrose was "betrayed not by false friends or incompetent subordinates, but by his own inability to grasp the importance of thorough reconnaissance" (Reid, 1990, 178). All generals need an element of luck – Montrose's luck had run out that April afternoon.

From Ardvreck the Marquis was taken to Skibo Castle where he remained for two nights and then taken to Tain where he was handed over to the magistrate who in turn passed him on to General Leslie. Although fevered and in pain Montrose, set upon a little Shetland pony with rags and straw as the saddle with his feet tied below the horse's belly, was taken from thence to Inverness. Crowds gathered to stare and jeer and the Provost is reputed to have said to him "My Lord, I am sorry for your circumstances" but Montrose simply replied "I am sorry for being the object of your pity." After a night at Castle Stewart he was taken south. His final destination was the scaffold at Edinburgh where he was hanged on 21 May 1650. He was aged thirty-eight. He would trouble Scotland no more.

He had been a great commander and he had met death bravely and with great dignity. In his last statement, spoken on the platform on which stood the gallows, there was no hint of bitterness –

> "I have no more to say, but that I desire your charity and prayers, I shall pray for you all. I leave my soul to God, my service to my prince, my goodwill to my friends, my love and charity to you all" (Buchan, 1928, 377).

We are told that tears ran down the face of the hangman and the crowd sobbed. They had put to death a man who more than any other Scottish hero had been that rare breed – 'a candidate for immortality' (Buchan, 1928, 382).

A later historian, Sir George Douglas, has commented that his execution by Covenanting leaders was an example of "the fiendish relish for saying off old scores which was strangely at odds with their lofty claims and sanctimonious profession" (*Glasgow Herald*, 14 April 1923) but that is an example of historiography with hindsight. The men of 1650 behaved as men of 1650 behaved and not how we think they ought to have behaved. The Age of the Covenanters has been called the 'Killing Times". Montrose was sadly one of its greatest victims.

Today the picturesque ruins of Ardvreck Castle, at the end of a rocky peninsula of Ard Bhreac, near the head of Loch Assynt, are a sombre if charming feature of this rugged countryside. When it was built in 1591 it must have been a most imposing castle but sadly its reputation as the last refuge of Montrose and his sorry demise thereafter has ensured that Ardvreck has the mark of shame upon it rather than that of pride.

Skibo Castle, on the other hand, had a remarkable renaissance in the early years of this century when Andrew Carnegie, the millionaire philanthropist, having acquired the estate spent a fortune on the massive reconstruction and enlargement of the modern castle which had replaced the one in which Montrose had been held. Under the hands of Messrs Ross and Macbeth, architects, it surely became one of the most lavish holiday homes of all time; indeed they had also to design a smaller house of Aultnagar to enable the Carnegies to truly get away from it all, Skibo having become almost another business headquarters. Now the business was about giving money away and not making more of it. Carnegie provided his Skibo with a 'Montrose Room' on its first floor for he had much admired the Marquis and one of the stained-glass lights to the staircase depicts the gallant hero. Skibo has had a chequered career since the Carnegie family moved out and plans are currently afoot to turn the Skibo estate into a major hotel development and thus perhaps many others will be able to enjoy its splendours.

The unpretentious, white-harled crow-stepped gabled building, known as 'The Ark', and possibly the home of the Sheriff, has fared worst of all. It had been the house where the Marquis lodged for the night when captive at Tain. After various uses it became a model lodging house before being demolished in 1940. Not even a plaque marks the site of the historic little house.

Heath's account of the battle records that it was at "Carbisdale" but the battle seems to have been earlier been labelled as 'of Invercharron'. Later, and for some reason unknown, it was renamed that 'of Carbisdale'. The 600 foot high hill overlooking the battlefield and from which Montrose had been tempted down had been given the name of 'Creag a Choinneachen' (rock of the mossy place) which had been mistranslated as Rock or Hill of Lamentation. It had however that name long before our battle and thus even if it did mean Rock of Lamentation – it was presumably so named because of an earlier battle, (possibly the Battle of Tuiteam – Tarbhach, between the Macleods and the Mackays, fought nearby and possibly in 1397). Highland history has never been short of lamentation.

The Battle of Carbisdale marked the beginning of the end of the Marquis. It also ensured that the name Carbisdale would linger forever in Scottish history.

CHAPTER TWENTY

Change And Decay

And come he slow, or come he fast,
It is but Death who comes at last.
SIR WALTER SCOTT – from *Marmion*

It had been a regular comment of Queen Victoria's that "the Queen wishes no changes".

When the Duchess died in 1912 her world was already passing rapidly into the realms of history and would be cast asunder by the Great War. She had been an attractive young lady who had blossomed into a celebrated Victorian *femme fatale* but who had mellowed into a rather sadly eccentric Edwardian Dowager-Duchess with a penchant for collecting property.

Although she had lived largely in the Victorian era she was essentially an Edwardian figure. In a sense much of the fun-loving Edwardian times had ran concurrently with the more prim Victorian ones even if in a strict historical sense the Edwardian era followed the Victorian one. It was an attitude of mind and way of life as much as tidy historical pigeon-holing.

The old Duke had been a great friend of the Prince of Wales and both knew how to indulge themselves in life's pleasures. The Duchess too had shared that hedonistic lifestyle. King Edward had died in 1910 at the age of sixty-eight whereas she died in 1912 at the age of sixty-four. They were as near contemporaries as makes no odds. They were both creatures of the same heart: both rejected the strict Victorian values; both were rebels and both were individuals.

Since Leeds' Clarendon Road, the main road of the area, had been named after the earls of Clarendon it seemed logical to apply their family name to another road; thus Hyde Terrace was so named. It was developed in rather piecemeal fashion during the nineteenth century. The site of what was to become Nos 9 – 13 was to be the final residential development of the street "having three enormous houses built on it" but they were not to stay private residences for long. By 1908 The Yorkshire Co-operative Nursing Home occupied the entire block.

Hyde having been a one- time student in her father's old college and having both lived at Hyde Park Place in London and inherited Hyde Farm near Taunton, it was surely somewhat ironical that the Duchess should find herself in Hyde Terrace. It was also strange that although the nursing home occupied the entire block from Nos 9-19 the Duchess was unlucky enough to be a patient in one of the grand rooms of No 13.

She had achieved great riches but perhaps as she lay on her sick bed she may have mused over Sir Walter's wise counsel: "All health is better than wealth". Comfortable though she was in this room it was a far cry from the luxuries of her home and houses. She was sadly to lose both health and wealth. As Scott has it "We maun aa die when our day comes", for the Dowager-Duchess her day had come. She died at Hyde Terrace on 25 May 1912. She had fought her last battle – cancer had won.

Although her family had historical links with the old Earls of Cromarty it had not been something that was highly regarded by Mary Caroline. What was the point of claiming long-forgotten kinship with a distant earl when she had herself become a great Duchess and even owned a sizeable piece of Ross-shire? Like almost all the Scottish aristocracy, before and since, she regarded herself as a cosmopolitan and metropolitan figure, not simply as a Highland estate owner. Any Scottish ties seem to have been held in justifiably limited regard. There was to be no hint of an old Scottish funeral;

indeed, she wanted a simple English funeral. Links that had maybe once been strong and had once maybe mattered had ceased to matter much by 1912.

In Robert Browning's 'My Last Duchess' his Duke lamented the fact that his wife had "ranked my gift of a 900 year old name/With anybody's gift", but not so Duchess Blair – she had revelled in being Duchess of Sutherland. The *Lady's Pictorial* had pointed out, perhaps rather cruelly, at the time of her wedding to Sir Albert that she would be simply Lady Rollit. She was never going to be simply Lady Rollit – she had been and would forever be the Duchess of Sutherland. She had once truly lived the part and now in death she wished to regain the role.

Macgregor has told of her marriage to the Duke as being "not a happy one" and that the Duke "rued the day he had met her" (Macgregor, 1965, 66). Duchess Anne's friend and confidante, Lady Paget, had stated of the Duchess Blair's marriage that "she led him a dog's life, but he, being weak could not extricate himself from her toils" (Paget, 1923, 539). There is no evidence to support Macgregor and Paget's unsubstantiated gossip. On the contrary, facts point in a different direction – a will which increased her share of the spoil would appear to suggest not a weakening but a strengthening in affection. If she had ever fallen out of love for the Duke then the evidence is slight in the extreme but of one fact there can be no dispute – she was in love with being the Duchess of Sutherland. If, in real life, marriage had strictly speaking made her Lady Rollit then she would certainly be buried as the Duchess of Sutherland.

One can never be quite sure whether the Dowager-Duchess had a boundless love for the Duke or simply an unending loathing for the Sutherland Family – in either account she was determined, out of love or spite, to be buried beside him. The Duke had stated in his will that she could be buried beside him at Trentham if she so wished. It was too tempting an offer to refuse. She therefore not only stipulated that she wished to be "buried by the side of her late husband . . . in the

Mausoleum at Trentham and beneath the same stone which covers his remains" but also that "I further desire that my coffin be made of either the thinnest wood or of osiers or of some material of the most perishable kind". She was determined to get as close as possible to the Duke.

She did not get quite all that she wanted. She was laid in an oak coffin. In death, as in life, it does not do to be too demanding!

Although she had often been spiteful in her life, she was in death generous to all her family, to some friends and loyal servants. All benefited by her will. Her daughter, of course, gained most. She acquired all the property.

Whether designed to reflect a new spirit of the age or just her weariness with men in general all her nephews and nieces were to gain from her estate but it was decreed that "nieces get double the amount awarded to nephews". She was, as we well know, a Duchess prone to be rather spiteful and to bear grudges, and indeed to bear them bitterly and long. For whatever reason young Norman Michell had riled her in the past she could not forgive him and thus all the other nieces and nephews benefited in her will "except Norman Michell". It did not pay to cross Duchess Blair. The head gardener and house-keeper at Carbisdale and other loyal servants were all generously provided for.

The Duchess and her deeds were long remembered but like much that is half remembered her exploits became distorted and confused. A dark picture of her has been painted. Macgregor has done a hatchet job on her. He has reported that his friend, Sandy, had claimed that Duchess Blair "waas a baad, baad butch" and recounted tales of her exploits which suggested "there existed no blacker Dowager in Christendom" (Macgregor, 1965, 62).

Certainly she had few redeeming qualities – she was domineering and headstrong, inflexible, impatient and intolerant, greedy and selfish, pig-headed and stubborn but one could more or less apply these adjectives to her 'foe', her stepson. She has been accused of being crafty but in order to achieve

what she regarded as her just deserts craft had been necessary. She has been depicted as a painted Jezebel whereas she
was in effect a widow at a loss how to come to terms with
bereavement as much as to how to handle a great legacy. She
may have shaped many of her circumstances but she may also
have been a victim of circumstances. Vindictive and spiteful
she may have been but it is difficult to ascertain whether this
was in her character or had simply been a response to the
vindictiveness of others.

The 4th Duke of Sutherland, "her innocent stepson" in
Macgregor's eyes, could not bring himself to even contem-
plate being buried beside either his father from whom he had
been so long estranged or the hated Duchess in the family
mausoleum at Trentham. He had taken steps, well before her
death, to ensure that his very own mausoleum would be built
at Dunrobin. He, of course, did not realise that he would not
long survive that Dowager whom he so detested. Less than a
year later he died and was buried in the new mausoleum. It is
a charming little building and had originally been a small
neo-classical temple-cum-summerhouse and had stood in
front of the Italianate splendours of Trentham Hall. It had
been one of Sir Charles Barry's creations and the Duke had it
removed stone by stone and re-erected on a spot of his own
choosing in the policies of Dunrobin.

He had been a quiet taciturn figure who never shared his
father's zest for life. Though like his father not academically
inclined he lacked his father's winsome ways; to be fair
though, Lady Paget considered him to be "the salt of the
earth" (Paget, 1923, 539).

Both the 3rd Duke who loved fires and Duchess Blair who
loved Dunrobin missed out in the blaze of 13 June 1915 which
destroyed much of the castle while in use as a military hospital during the Great War. The Dunrobin Fire Brigade could
not cope and Inverness had to dispatch its brigade by train. At
its peak almost 1000 men were at work combatting the flames
(*Scotsman*, 14 June 1915). Although all the wounded men were
got out safely a young officer in the Territorials was seriously

injured when the roof on which he was standing gave way. Old Dr Simpson, of fond memory, had him speedily taken to the local hospital.

When Sir Robert Lorimer came to restore the castle it was remodelled and shorn of some of Barry's delightful fairy- tale towers and turrets. Lorimer brought Dunrobin back to earth – perhaps the fire truly did symbolically mark the end of an epoch.

That old chronicler of high-life, the octogenarian Lady Dorothy Nevill, had complained in her reminiscences of 1906 that wealth "had usurped the place formerly held by wit and learning" and the question now asked was no longer "Is So-and- so clever?" but instead "Is So-and-so rich?" (Read, 1972, 46). The Duke was indeed rich but without any real wit and learning while the Dowager-Duchess was essentially one of the new breed of aristocrats who had purchased her great estate to further bolster her social pretensions (Read, 1972, 46).

Henry Chaplin, the widower of Lady Florence, served as an MP for many years and in 1916 was elevated to the Lords as Viscount Chaplin. He had long enjoyed being called 'squire' by all and sundry although by 1892 his gambling had got him into such deep financial trouble that he was compelled to sell his family seat of Blankney Hall. *The Times* reckoned he was "one of the old school – almost the last example of the old landed gentry" (*The Times*, 9 May 1923). When he died in 1923 in Londonderry House, the home of his daughter, wife of the Marquis of Londonderry, his death reflected the passing of an age. In the very fulsome tribute given in *The Times* there was a very intriguing statement about Chaplin. It stated

> he was the hero or the victim of a historical romance and the manner in which he was revenged on his supplanter was a extra-ordinarily appropriate stroke of poetic justice. (*The Times*, 9 May 1923).

It is the sort of thing that begs further enquiry. One felt almost compelled to know more.

It seems that Henry Chaplin had become engaged to Lady

Florence Paget but the Marquess of Hastings had eloped with Chaplin's fiancee just before their planned wedding. It was to lead to a bitter feud, but Chaplin was to be revenged. Hastings was an even more reckless gambler than his rival and the more Chaplin backed his horse, Hermit, the heavier Hastings backed against it. Chaplin's horse, at 66 to 1, won the 1867 Derby winning for its owner a sizeable fortune but it also financially ruined Hastings. Chaplin in 1876 married Lady Florence, the daughter of the 3rd Duke of Sutherland, but as we know her early death robbed him of his wife after only five years of marriage.

However, let us return to the fate of Duchess Blair's property following her death.

After a few years Kinsbury Manor was sold, and likewise the Willows, but Duchess Blair's daughter, Irene, retained Carbisdale. The trustees of her mother's estate had the building completed and although it had been in part occupied as a hospital during the Great War Irene had its interiors completed not long afterwards. It was also suitably furnished in the grand manner.

Just as the exterior gives the illusion of a building of different dates so also does the interior. It is designed to convey the impression that differing styles reflect different periods of creation. The Age of Adam is celebrated in the drawing room while the Jacobean world is savoured in the library; that of the Baroque in the hall and that of the Tudor in its great staircase.

Let us go inside and see!

Through the *porte-cochère* one enters at the base of its lofty tower.

Upon entering one finds oneself in a large hall (now rather marred by modern 'improvements') but in its day boasting a rich collection of arms and armour from many countries. This in turn leads to the reception hall or lower gallery some 100 feet long with richly ornate Baroque chimney-piece decorated with a galaxy of figures and foliage. But it is the staggering collection of white Italian marble figures which takes one's breath away. The windows of this gallery overlook the courtyard. At the far end is located the dining room with its hand-made Japanese wallpaper (a firm favourite for clients of Messrs Shoolbred), its exquisite panelled dado, its great welcoming fire and collection of family portraits. It is a room some 36 feet by 31 feet in size. From the hall a great, wide, Tudor oak-carved, balustraded staircase leads to the upper floor and it is lit by the stained-glass windows depicting the Sutherland family history. It might have only been briefly Duchess Blair's family history but it will be a link which will remain as long as Carbisdale survives. Everywhere, fine panelled doors set in richly moulded doorcases can be seen and overhead are splendid plaster ceilings. Off the lower hall are also located the drawing room and library. The library has a rich Jacobean ceiling and carved wood Jacobean-style chim-neypiece as well as a fine collection of books set in splendid break-fronted bookcases. A finely-proportioned room with its bay windows overlooking the Dornoch Firth, it was luxuri-ously furnished with an abundance of leather chairs and sofas and a liberal sprinkling of reading lamps while the drawing room is unmistakingly Adamesque.

The upper gallery had housed the castle's great pipe organ, and, at one end, a raised dais – the twentieth-century equiva-lent of the minstrel's gallery – was used by the orchestra which played when the ballroom was in full swing. The Orchestrelle Company's Aeolian Pipe Organs were advertised as offering "the sweetest voices of the ancient and modern orchestra in all its greatest musical masterpieces". Carbisdale may have been remote from London but it was not meant to be remote from life's pleasures!

Carbisdale might simply be dismissed as a major landmark and somewhat derided but there is no question that internally it has craftsmanship of the highest order.

Irene Mary Blair, the Dowager-Duchess's daughter by her first husband, the unfortunate Arthur Kindersley Blair, had herself married in 1901. Her Prince Charming was an Austrian nobleman, Johann Franz, Count Bubna, and they had married in Windsor. There were to be two children, both girls – Olga, born in 1902, and Ina in 1903. Bubna was a talented, if little-known artist, etcher and lithographer. The marriage did not last however and they separated in 1908. Bubna seems to have preferred the more Bohemian life of Paris to the rather staid conventions of Brighton where they had briefly settled.

According to Macgregor the Countess "though not so attractive as her mother, was an infinitely finer woman" although she had "a marked degree of torticollis – of wry neck – however" (Macgregor, 1965, 66).

Irene may not have been like her mother in looks but she seemed nonetheless to have acquired some of her mother's traits. Like her mother she rather liked being a noblewoman and therefore for the rest of her life remained Countess Bubna. Unlike Duchess Blair, Countess Bubna was not a great acquirer of property and although she chiefly resided in London she seems to have been unable to settle and, in quick succession, had several houses. Firstly she lived at Manor House, Marylebone Road, then after a spell in Jermyn Street, Westminster, moved to Cork Street in fashionable Mayfair and then to Piccadilly, before settling at Bolton Studios, Redclyffe Square, Kensington. She also, for a spell, stayed at Kinsbury Manor, the home of her mother. With such an unsettled existence it perhaps comes as little surprise to find that her last known residence truly reflects her near nomadic lifestyle. It perhaps also suggests her liking for the exotic as well as her love of travel for she had the splendid Villa Amenadus at Luxor on the banks of the Nile and it was there that she died in the late 1920s or early 30s. It also seems likely that Count Bubna himself died in 1925 and as daughter Ina became the real Countess Bubna – her mother presumably becoming the Dowager-Countess – it is to be assumed that the elder daughter, Olga, had also died.

Countess Bubna, Duchess Blair's daughter, had frequently holidayed at Carbisdale. Writing in 1965, Alasdair Alpin Macgregor could recall her visits and Macgregor's Aunt Dorothy and the Countess seem to have been on amicable

terms and "sometimes encountered one another when shop-
ping or entertaining at Ardgay" (Macgregor, 1965, 66). On her
death the property was sold and it is believed that it was sold
only after being on the market for some time. Although much
interest was shown, prospective buyers for inexplicable
reasons opted out.

In March 1933 Mr Alastair Ronald Mackenzie of
Invergordon bought Carbisdale for £2000 and yet later that
year strangely sold it again. It was acquired by Lt. Col.
Theodore Salvesen, the senior partner in the whaling and
shipowning company, Messrs Christian Salvesen & Co. and
director of the other companies which together formed the
great enterprise known as Salvesen of Leith. The Salvesens
had come to Edinburgh from Norway in the 1850s and
though they had begun in shipbroking had grown and prospered to become owners of a mighty merchant fleet and one
of the world's leading whalers. They had also become familiar
figures in the Edinburgh Establishment.

Theodore was a warm- hearted figure but behind his genial
facade lurked a shrewd and able businessman. He was quick
and decisive and liked to take calculated risks and seize
opportunities as they arose. Carbisdale was possibly one of
the opportunities of a lifetime and he acquired it for a mere
£1,500. It was surely a bargain by any standard!

Col. Salvesen's grandson was later to recall that family
tradition had it that both the house and furniture were said to
have cost £12,000. It may be that £10,500 had to be paid for the
rich collection of furniture, paintings and statuary which had
so transformed Carbisdale from being simply a big castle into
the great country seat of the Duchess of Sutherland.

Salvesen's brother Edward had, as a young Counsel, acted
for Duchess Blair in her battle with the Sutherland family in
the Scottish courts. He would never have forgotten her forceful personality and probably advised his brother on the ducal
magnificence of Carbisdale Castle. It had been a home fit for a
Duchess – it was certainly a home fit for a wealthy tycoon.
The Salvesens had become successfully integrated into the

higher echelons of Scottish society but perhaps true arrival demanded a prestigious country estate? What could be grander than the former home of the Duchess of Sutherland?

As in so many familes the Great War extracted a heavy penalty. The Salvesen family was no exception. Theodore's brother, Thomas, was hardest hit. Two sons and a son-in-law were victims. His eldest son, Christian, was killed in the rail disaster at Quintinshill when a troop train taking soldiers bound for Gallipoli to Liverpool was in collision with two other trains. 215 men of the Royal Scots were to die in the carnage in Dumfriesshire rather than on the battlefields of the Dardanelles. Eric Salvesen died on the Western Front in 1917. In memory of his two sons, Thomas provided money for the erection of two homes for Scottish war veterans while Christian's house at Trinity was given by the family to the Royal Navy Benevolent Fund to be used as an orphan home. During the war it served as a convalescent home for wounded soldiers. This spirit of public service and acts of generosity were to remain a characteristic trait of the Salvesens.

Noel Salvesen, Theodore's eldest son, was severely wounded in the War although he later recovered sufficiently to act as Intelligence Officer and Military Control Officer for Scottish ports. His other two sons also served their country – the youngest, Norman, began as a naval cadet and was present at the surrender of the German fleet while Harold rose to the rank of Captain in the Indian Army and served with distinction in Mesopotamia, Persia, and in what was to become the Soviet Union.

Col. Salvesen was a big, expansive man. A charming and considerate host, he enjoyed entertaining and did so in sumptuous fashion. He lived life to the full and was great fun. The story is told how, no matter who was residing in the castle as his guest, he would each evening before retiring for the night pat the marble bottoms of all the ladies on their plinths of the hall at Carbisdale. These ladies did not complain!

Carbisdale probably for the first time in its life was witnessing laughter and happiness.

CHAPTER TWENTY-ONE

A Royal Interlude –
A Safe Refuge

Tramp! Tramp! along the land they rode,
Splash! Splash! along the sea.
SIR WALTER SCOTT – from *William and Helen*

One supposes that ideally castles are not worthy of the name unless they have royal connections. The more princes and princesses associated with them the better and better still the more regal the connection – witness the number of them that are romantically linked with the tragic figures of Mary, Queen of Scots, and Bonnie Prince Charlie, the Young Pretender. Many others boast of having rooms associated with Queen Victoria and even Dunrobin has its very own Queen Victoria's bedroom. Indeed the Sutherlands were so proud of the fact that Victoria stayed there in 1872 that after the disastrous fire on 13 June 1915 had destroyed much of the castle, including the royal apartments, it was rebuilt with the new rooms taking the old names. So although Queen Victoria never stayed in the room, only on the site of the room, it still bears her name and has her gilt four- poster bed in it.

Carbisdale cannot claim any link with Victoria, but nevertheless it too has its own royal connections. Like everything else about Carbisdale there is a story attached to it as well.

Although Norway had seen much of its merchant shipping destroyed the country had managed to stay out of World War One. Norway was not to be allowed that luxury with the advent of the Second World War. On 9 April 1940 Germany launched a surprise attack on the country and although military resistance lasted for sixty-two days – longer than any other country except the USSR – the Nazi war machine triumphed in the end.

King Haakon VII endeavoured to hold his government together by his own courage, determination and endurance. The government were forced to flee from Oslo and when the Luftwaffe bombed the town in which they were staying they were compelled to move again. The king was "chased from village to village and from cottage to cottage" (*Scotsman*, 6 June 1945) and in a strenuous journey through the deep snow of the Norwegian mountains he was "harried by air attack and nearly captured by German parachutists" (*Glasgow Herald*, 23 September 1957).

Having managed to evade German land and air forces they reached Molde but it was already in flames as a result of German bombing. When the Allies were forced to evacuate from the South of Norway the king decided he would head north and thus sailed aboard the British cruiser HMS *Glasgow* from Andalsnes to Tromso where he hoped to stay and lead Norwegian resistance against the occupying force.

The ship too was attacked from the air. Norway was increasingly becoming too dangerous a place in which to remain and the allies were soon forced to evacuate from Narvik. On 7 June, the anniversary of the dissolution of the union with Sweden which resulted in Norway becoming independent, it was reluctantly decided that Norway must make another historic step – the government and King must go into exile to Britain and from there direct their country's continuing struggle against the enemy.

At the last cabinet meeting held in Norway the King stated

> It may seem as if today's decision means the abandoning of the freedom that was gained in 1905. But we believe that in taking the decision forced upon us today, we have taken the only decision possible if we are to uphold all that was accomplished on that date. (*Scotsman*, 5 June 1945).

King Haakon sailed from Tromso on board the British cruiser HMS *Devonshire*.

Although he was to be ostensibly deposed by the Nazis during his exile he never ceased to command the respect and loyalty of his people and he remained not only their leader but became the symbol of his country's freedom. Before the war, Vidkum Quisling had headed the miniscule Facist party, Nasjonal Samling, but when Hitler appointed General Torboven as his Commisar in Norway he invited Quisling to head the puppet government. In accepting the role, Quisling provided a name which will be for ever synonymous with the political collaborator. After the war Quisling was shot as a traitor.

King Haakon was no stranger to London – he had been married in Buckingham Palace to his cousin, Princess Maud, the sister of the Prince of Wales (the future King George V). As Prince Charles of Denmark he was a grandson of Queen Victoria and was thus a great- uncle to Queen Elizabeth II. He was also the first sovereign to rule over the independent kingdom of Norway when it was established in 1905. In Norway he dispensed with much of the regal pomp and made himself a popular 'people's king'.

At first the king settled in Bowdown House, near Newbury, but as a large military aerodrome was to be established at nearby Greenham Common it was considered that a house with less potential danger from enemy bombing might be a safer refuge. It was also considered desirable that the King's house should be near London. It was perhaps not surprising that he should therefore choose to stay at Foliejohn Park, near Windsor – for not only was it an elegant late eighteenth-century country house set in parkland complete with five-acre lake but it was a site with a long history.

It had once belonged to the crown and been the one-time seat of the constables of Windsor Castle. More recently, Princess Hatzfeldt-Wildenberg, the widow of one of the Hapsburgs – the Austrian imperial family – had lived there for many years and had entertained lavishly. It was almost within a stone's throw of one of the King's old haunts – Windsor Castle – and within an hour's drive from London.

Foliejohn Park was therefore the surrogate Norwegian capital for most of the war. The King and his son occupied the right wing of the house with the King's private study on the ground floor and the room, overlooking the swimming pool, was long known as the 'King's bedroom'. One of the King's favourite pastimes was to have long walks in the 500 acres of the estate. A plaque in the hall of the house proudly states "During the German occupation of Norway H.M. King Haakon VII resided in this house".

The King remained at Foliejohn until it was safe to return home. After Norway was liberated on 8 May 1945 the long-hoped for dream became reality. King Haakon was the first of Europe's exiled monarchs to return home and he was given a rousing and heroic welcome. On 7 June 1945 50,000 spectators were at Oslo ready to greet him and his home- coming was a triumphal progression. His motto had been "All for Norway" and the well- wishers roared this greeting at their much loved King. He was glad to be home – they were glad to have him home.

During their exile the King and Crown Prince did much to encourage the Norwegian forces stationed in this country and as many of these men were based in Scotland there were accordingly many Royal visits to Scotland. Many Norwegians had arrived via the 'Shetland Bus', a shuttle service of small vessels which picked up Norwegians from under the noses of their Nazi overlords and brought them safely, if dangerously, across the North Sea to Shetland. From there the men made their way to the mainland and joined their compatriots in the various branches of the Norwegian services.

On one of his visits to Scotland the King visited and officially opened the school which had been established in Drumochty Castle near Stonehaven. The castle had become a residential school for Norwegian refugee children and most of its seventy pupils had come from Norway since the occupation had begun – some had arrived in boats with their parents while others had been uplifted in British warships after successful allied commando raids on Vaagso and the Lofoten Islands. One of the little boys in the school had been a stowaway. His father had planned to escape from Norway but due to the risks involved considered it best to leave his wife and children behind. With nightfall he made his getaway in a fishing boat but once it was out to sea a small boy crept out from beneath a tarpaulin and proudly declared "Here I am, father!" (*Glasgow Herald*, 2 November 1942).

Many of the staff had also managed to escape from Norway after the Nazis had taken possession of their homeland.

King Haakon and Crown Prince Olav were personal friends of Lord Salvesen and his brother Col. T. E. Salvesen, the Honorary Norwegian Consul from 1926 to 1939, and when they were in Scotland on their tour of inspection of Norwegian forces they resided either at Lord Salvesen's Edinburgh home – Dean Park House – or in the summer at Col. Salvesen's holiday residence at Carbisdale. This they did in the summer of 1942 and possibly at other times. Although there is no brass plate in the hall to record their stay, bedrooms in the castle are still affectionately known as 'King Haakon's Room' and 'Prince Olav's Room'. The King also no doubt enjoyed the strolls around the attractive estate policies and enjoyed the magnificent views from the library and drawing room windows. He may have liked the view from his bedroom at Foliejohn Park but the view from his bedroom at Carbisdale was perfect and somewhere in the distance lay his beloved Norway.

Among the many places in Scotland which they visited to inspect Norwegian forces was nearby Dornoch and in front of Dornoch Cathedral a tree was planted to commemorate the visit. King Haakon also on one occasion went to see the Queen's View at Loch Tummel – perhaps someone had told him of the connection between Carbisdale and the 'murder' at Tummel Bridge!

Just as King Haakon's stay at Foliejohn Park, for security

reasons, had received little or no publicity, neither did his times at Carbisdale. It has proved an impossible task trying to piece together his activities but one major event which was most secret at the time but which had major repercussions for the future did take place during one of his visits to Carbisdale. The castle was the venue for a most historic meeting when King Haakon presided over what was to be termed the 'Carbisdale Conference'. It seems likely that others present included Crown Prince Olav, the Norwegian Chiefs of Staff including their Commander-in-Chief General Carl Fleischer, while British delegates consisted of General (later Sir) Andrew Thorne, the GOC in C Scottish Command and Governor of Edinburgh Castle, and Col. Sir John Aird of the General Staff and an Equerry to King George VI, and of course Col. Salvesen himself. The conference led to an agreement between the Allied Powers that when victory came Norway should again become an independent state. This agreement was honoured by all parties and even although Russian forces were to enter Norway on 25 October 1944 and sweep the German 28th (Lapland) Army from Norway and capture at least thirty towns the Red Army nevertheless withdrew at the end of hostilities. Norway was not liberated from the Germans simply to remain in Soviet hands and become enmeshed in the bleak Soviet bloc which for so long had been the fate of Eastern Europe but instead it joined the free nations of the world. It is perhaps little wonder Carbisdale has had such a strong appeal to Norwegian visitors to this day.

General Thorne had been Governor of historic Edinburgh Castle – one wonders what he made of the new Carbisdale Castle? He certainly contributed to its history. He was to become Commander-in-Chief of the Allied Land Forces in Norway and was to head the SHAEF Mission to Norway in 1945. Norway was to be very grateful for his services and he was to be honoured and fêted in return. He received the Grand Cross of the Order of St Olav as well as their Freedom Medal. Col. Aird was not forgotten – he received the Order of King Olav. Both men and a historic meeting at Carbisdale had contributed much to Norway's freedom.

Lord Salvesen and his wife had a Norwegian home, Risobank, where they delighted to entertain. Risobank became a "byword for hospitality" and when guests arrived at the port of Christiansand the Customs Officer would tell them "You will have a good time there" (Andorson, 1949, 226). One imagines that the same good measure of hospitality would be on offer at both Carbisdale and Dean Park and the Norwegian Royal Family would have been regally entertained.

When he had been alive he had actively befriended many Norwegian refugees and thus it was appropriate that when Col. Salvesen died, his home at Edinburgh's Inverleith Place was given to the Free Norway forces and became known as Norway House.

When King Haakon arrived in Edinburgh on his way to Rosyth for his homeward journey one of the people to greet him at Waverley station was Mr Norman Salvesen, the Norwegian Consul in Edinburgh. The Honorary Norwegian Consulate in Edinburgh had been established in 1906, probably the first of such consulates to be established and for fifty years the Salvesen family provided these consuls. The Salvesens provided a strong link between Norway and Scotland. Carbisdale is a lasting memorial to that bond of friendship between these two countries.

CHAPTER TWENTY-TWO

From Spite Castle to Youth Hostel

To all, to each, a fair good night,
And pleasing dreams, and slumbers light.
SIR WALTER SCOTT – from Marmion

Colonel Salvesen's brother was to rise through the ranks of the legal profession to become Lord Salvesen, the distinguished High Court judge. He was a man of wide-ranging interests, including Edinburgh Zoo (the Scottish National Zoological Park) for which he devoted much effort. Perhaps his greatest interest, however, was the Scottish Youth Hostels Association of which he became the first President. The SYHA seemed to embrace the things Salvesen loved most – walking, countryside and open air – and to encourage others to share in these enjoyments seemed the most laudable of aims.

He was to be no mere figurehead for he "threw himself into the work of furthering the project with all his accustomed vigour" (Andorson, 1949, 218). He presided over the public meeting in Edinburgh which inaugurated the movement on 13 February 1931. He officially opened the first hostel at Old Broadmeadow at Yarrow in the Scottish Borders on 2 May that year. Broadmeadows had been a row of four farm workers' cottages but was converted to a hostel, capable of housing twenty-nine. Salvesen declared it was "the aim of the association . . . to have a chain of hostels throughout the whole of Scotland" (*Glasgow Herald*, 4 May 1931). Although he headed the subscription lists and cajoled his family into supporting it with money, the public response during the troubled 'Thirties' was far from generous for this new venture. But

slow as the money was to come in, the movement nevertheless grew. By the late summer four hostels had been established in the Borders. There were to be a total of nine hostels
at the end of the first year and by April 1933 there were nine-
teen hostels ready to receive guests and the Association had
4000 members on its roll (*The Times*, 18 April 1933).
Subscriptions had been deliberately set low to encourage as
wide a membership as possible – 2/6 for those under twenty-
five years of age and 5/- for those over. It was perhaps little
wonder that Sir J. M. Barrie writing in 1933 (at the age of
seventy- three) declared "the enterprise makes me wish I was
a Scottish youth again" (*The Times*, 16 April 1933).

Salvesen had seen the SYHA develop from having four
hostels to having fifty hostels within a few years. Although
many of its properties were unostentatiously described as
"timber buildings" its properties ranged from castles and
mansion houses to simple cottages. Salvesen believed hiking
should appeal to everyone and from all walks of life; with the
ever increasing use of the motor car he feared people "might
lose the art of walking". Walking was, in his view "the only
form of exercise one could indulge in from the age of one to
the age of ninety-nine" (*Scotsman*, 24 February 1942). The
Youth Hostels were about walking and fresh air.

The association's other president was Sir John Stirling
Maxwell of Pollok and he, for many years, had been a neigh-
bour of the Dowager-Duchess of Sutherland, having his
London home in Belgrave Square. In the 1930s he was
Chairman of the Forestry Commission as well as owning
extensive estates. He gave the use of the boathouse at Loch
Ossian, part of his Corrour estate, for use as another hostel.
The Carnegie Trust provided money for a hostel at Inverbeg
on Loch Lomondside and the Marquis of Lothian granted the
use of historic Ferniehirst Castle in the Borders. The Scottish
Youth Hostels continued to expand. By 1939 there were 20,000
members and its sixty-four hostels provided accommodation
totalling 3,548 beds.

Lord Salvesen had died barely a month after his brother

Lt.Col. Theodore Salvesen in the winter of 1942. Col. Salvesen's son inherited Carbisdale and would seem to have had little desire to retain it. Although it is said he tried to sell it or give the castle away with a war raging and an uncertain future it would not be the best time to get hold of a purchaser or even find a recipient. These may simply have been unfounded rumours, for the final destiny of the castle was fairly easily and not too surprisingly secured. The family had long been renowned for their philanthropy and giving Carbisdale away would simply be another act of benevolence on a truly grand scale.

Although he did not live to see it one expects that Lord Salvesen would have been well pleased when his nephew, Captain Harold Salvesen, an Honorary Vice-President of the SYHA, presented another castle to add to its property portfolio – the spectacular Carbisdale Castle. It was to be, and indeed remains, its largest and grandest hostel. Comparing it with the other hostels one commentator noted "Carbisdale Castle provides a majestic contrast with these humble wayside quarters" (*Scottish Field*, January 1945).

Writing in 1932 Professor Alexander Gray of Aberdeen University pleaded for "a few men of substance" to each provide a hostel, and in so doing "they would not merely erect a memorial which would save their name from oblivion, but they would likewise further a cause which . . . may well prove one of the great beneficent factors in the formation of (future) generations" (*Scots Magazine*, 1932, 86). Captain Salvesen was indeed a 'man of substance' who has ensured a lasting memorial by aiding succeeding generations in discovering the Highlands of Scotland.

A photograph on a wall of the drawing room is the sole expression of the indebtedness of the SYHA to Capt. Salvesen but he was a man who did not look for glory and delighted in service. He would have been pleased that his castle still served real needs and remained a safe and magnificent refuge for overseas visitors as well as resident Scots seeking to enjoy fresh air and the Scottish countryside.

Carbisdale was opened as a hostel on Saturday 2 June 1945 and it is interesting to note that on the previous day the Norwegian Government held its State council in Oslo – the first time since 1940. Carbisdale had had a role to play in achieving Norway's future as a free nation.

When first opened it had been the aim that the large galleries of the Castle be used for musical recitals and for cinema shows and that some rooms be used to illustrate the life and development of Northern Scotland. These ideas seem to have been overlooked of late but a welcome recent innovation is that on certain afternoons visitors can join an organised tour of the house. It is too grand a place and too major a part of our history for it simply to be left to hostellers to enjoy. Carbisdale Castle was built to be enjoyed and ought to be made available for the enjoyment of many.

Unlike almost every other youth hostel, Carbisdale has an art collection that many a country house would be glad to possess. It was a collection chiefly gathered by the Dowager-Duchess of Sutherland and includes around eighty paintings, many reflecting aspects of her life and times. One painting is of Boveney Lock on the Thames, more or less just across from where Duchess Blair had her home at the Willows near Windsor. Some paintings are, not surprisingly, of her one-time home – Dunrobin Castle and its grounds – and for a Duchess fond of gardening there are scenes of both the gardens at Trentham as well as Dunrobin. Another depicts the mine at Trentham while others are of well-known beauty spots on the Sutherland estates – Strath Kildonan, Loch Assynt and Lochinver. Carbisdale Castle itself features in one work while other paintings reflect her more exotic interests and love of travel – Egypt and Venice. It is, however, the array of marble statuary that is quite breathtaking. Little wonder Col. Salvesen was wont to caress them – the hall has surely one of the finest sculpture collections of any great house. Some are by unknown Italian hands while a few are by such distinguished Scottish home-grown sculptural talent as D. W. Stevenson and Lawrence Macdonald.

The art collection more than proves that Duchess Blair may not have been short of money but equally she was not short of artistic appreciation.

The SYHA are as immensely proud of their castle as they are of its art collection. Their leaflet outlining its history describes it as "the Association's most splendid property". The seafaring Salvesens would no doubt find real satisfaction in the fact that Carbisdale has become, without doubt, the flagship of their fleet.

The Castle is deservedly popular with hostellers. In few castles can one have the opportunity to sleep in a room once used by a real king. Few hostels have upwards of 200 rooms. Carbisdale Castle is such a hostel.

It has had a brief but glamorous history. Few twentieth-century buildings have a comparable story and few aristocratic fortunes have been as spectacularly won and wasted as that of the House of Sutherland. Carbisdale is part of that rich story. It is also a fine building built by a fascinating woman.

All's Well That Ends. . .

Whose heart hath ne'er within him burn'd,
As home his footsteps he hath turn'd
From wandering on a foreign strand!
SIR WALTER SCOTT – from *The Lay of the Last Minstrel*

Real castles have ghosts or so we are led to believe. We could scarcely end an account of Carbisdale Castle – the last real castle to be built in Scotland – without mentioning its ghosts.

Macgregor has told of an old man he knew who

> "heard pipes playing under what, today, is the castle's rocky site. What an unseen piper was doing there, he could not imagine, though he felt sure these unaccountable strains foretold great changes in the locality (Macgregor, 1952)

Shortly afterwards men came to blast the rock in order to build the foundations of the castle.

MacGregor has claimed that "the playing of phantom bagpipes could be heard on other occasions, but apart from the phantom pipe music there was also supposed to be phantom organ music. The ghostly organist presumably was playing the organ in the castle ballroom.

George Murray, later employed in the gardens of Carbisdale, was reported to have looked up one summer's day and there standing beside a whin-bush in front of him was

> the figure of a lady clad in white dress which seemed to fall as if draped from her shoulders. In a nonce she was

gone. George proceeded instantly to the spot where he had seen her but could find no one there, nor anything to explain matters (MacGregor, 1965, 57).

Two or three times that summer Murray reputedly saw the apparition and it was also seen by at least two others. A warden of the hostel who was rather sceptical of Carbisdale's ghost was later to say that he could see the logical sense in "the famous lady in white" who is supposed to wander around the castle from time to time. It would not take too much imagination to conclude that the lady in white was none other than poor Duchess Blair who had not lived to see her castle completed.

At least one of the hostel's wardens and his wife, together with many hostellers, claim to have had experiences of the supernatural and many of these experiences seem to tie in with the history of the castle.

The Willows and nearby Sutherland Grange have been converted into flats. The grounds of the Willows which had been a favourite haunt of travellers in the past now serve a new public – they have become a popular caravan park and in the middle of it is a charming little black and white building – known as King Edward Cottage. Now apparently used rather pragmatically as a little shop it may have had a more august role in the past. No one knows quite when it first gained that name but it may well have had a most important and yet unknown connection with the Prince of Wales or it may simply have been so named in honour of his involvement in the settlement of the great Sutherland Will Case. It remains a tangible if tantalisingly mysterious link to those dramatic days.

The Sutherland family had to retrench and reform. The English properties fared particularly badly although no part remained untouched by changing circumstances as much as by death duty.

In 1910, estate agents Messrs Knight Frank and Rutley were instructed to sell the 1200 acres of Stittenham. It had been where our story of the Gower family had begun – now it was destined to pass into other hands.

Trentham had been the first casualty of a process of erosion which, like a cancer, quickly spread. The family stopped using it and in late 1906 the contents of the library were auctioned and in July of 1907 pictures, furniture and other contents were sold. The Duke offered the Hall to Staffordshire County Council as a college but as he was unhappy about it being used for training female teachers the idea fell through. He later offered it as an art gallery or museum for the Potteries but the offer was refused in view of the likely probable costs of its conversion and maintenance. Nobody seemed to want Trentham and without love it had no future. The palatial mansion was largely demolished but enough of its glory remains to give a taste of what it all might have been like in its day – quite grand amid a superb setting. Its delightful gardens are open regularly and part of the estate has become a caravan park so people can still visit and stay in Trentham even if they cannot stay at Trentham Hall. Trentham Parish Church still happily serves its lively congregation as well as providing a home for some handsome Sutherland memorials.

The Italianate top of the tower of Trentham was sold for about £100 to Lord Harrowby and was re-erected in the grounds of Sandon Hall as a charming belvedere. It remains one of the most delightful little buildings to be found in any English garden.

In February 1912 the Duke of Sutherland told his tenants at Lilleshall that he proposed to sell 8,500 acres and that he was willing to lend them money to finance their mortgages should they wish to purchase what was considered to be "some of best agricultural land in the country" (*The Times*, 3 February 1912). In 1914 his son, the 5th Duke, sold another eight farms and a total of 2,500 acres.

Although Lilleshall had acquired a new billiard room wing in 1906 it did not remain long in Sutherland family owner-ship. It was sold after the Great War and was later to become a National Sports Centre having been purchased by the South African Government and gifted to Britain in 1950. Extensive buildings have since been added to provide for all manner of indoor games activities while the grounds provide a range of outdoor sporting facilities.

In November 1912 the 4th Duke, though he had resented any prospect of his father relinquishing Stafford House was himself willing to yield it. He sold Stafford House to Sir William Hesketh Lever, later Lord Leverhulme, who declared he would put it "to some public or national use" (*The Times*, 13 November 1912) and he in fact presented it to the nation. Renamed Lancaster House it has now become a palatial government reception venue.

Magnificent Cliveden which the 3rd Duke had sold to his brother-in-law, the Duke of Westminster, in 1870, has perhaps fared best of all of former Sutherland properties. It was in 1893 sold to the fabulously rich William Waldorf Astor in whose family it remained, serving dutifully as a hospital during the two World Wars but also acquiring a reputation for high life. The gardens and house were then gifted to the National Trust. The gardens and grounds remain open to the public while the house has become one of the grandest of country-house hotels.

In the spring of 1914 the properties at Tittensor extending to 1276 acres were put on the market. The entire village was up for sale as was delightful Tittensor Chase with its famous fish ponds. The family of Richard Copeland were able to obtain the house which only thirty years earlier had caused so much fuss.

During the Second World War the Clearing Banks rather ironically cleared out of London. They settled in at Trentham, well away, or so they hoped, from German bombers and other dangers. To commemorate their time at Trentham a monument was erected and it is a large five-sided bronze sculpture, symbolic of a very large fifty-pence. It is apposite that the banks should wish to leave a representation of money to remind us of their days there. It also seems appropriate in the light of our tale for money was to cause so much trouble to the House of Sutherland.

The Mausoleum at Trentham is today a sadly neglected,

even if impressive, monument. With a backcloth of bushes
and trees and set a few yards from the busy A34 its bold and
powerful lines seem constrained and restricted. Sadly it has
also been vandalised. Handles are missing from its otherwise
mighty iron door furniture and a cheap padlock, miraculously
and miserably even if effectively, holds the intruder at bay.
Rich moulding and panelling on the door has been replaced
with plywood sheeting. There is little evidence of its once
magnificent stained glass and wire mesh has been a more
recent substitute. Lichen and moss green the walls and tree
and plant sprout proudly and uncaringly from the walls. If
man does not care why should nature!

The massive stone blocks and battered walls of the
mausoleum were a creation of the 1st Duke of Sutherland and
his architect, J. A. Tatham, and it is among the finest
mausoleum buildings in England. This was celebration of
death on a grand scale. The maintenance of the lavish memorial was however sadly overlooked in the calculation. Survival
is as necessary a component as creation in the art of commem-
oration and Trentham is a prime example of a situation where
future generations were unable or unwilling to take on the
cost of maintaining such a building.

The gardener tending the well-trimmed lawns of the adjacent cemetery reported that some years ago the bodies in the
mausoleum had been exhumed; presumably because vandals,
time and the climate had rendered the mausoleum an unsafe
refuge for the deceased. Rumour has it that the bodies were
reinterred in the family burial ground at Dunrobin – it would
have been a fitting end for 'Duchess Blair' if she did after all
end up in Sutherland.

The Countess of Sutherland has, however, given her assur-
ance that no bodies have been taken from the mausoleum, so
presumably the 3rd Duke and his Duchess still lie together in
what little peace the vandal permits.

The Sutherland Manor Estate in Florida fell on hard times.
Nothing now remains to recall the Sutherlands' stay in
Tarpon Springs. For a time some rubble of broken plaster and

bricks was strewn over the hillside. The house had been rented for a time but then, when finally deserted, it became a refuge for many squatters. In 1943 the land was sold to Mrs J. K. Chaney and the timber of the house purchased by Mr W. J. Meyer. By 1977 it was reported that about forty homes now occupied the site of the old Dukedom.

Our story began in Sutherland and it is there that we must return.

It had been planned to sell parts of the Sutherland estates in October 1914 but the sale had to be postponed due to the onset of the Great War. The sale was re-scheduled for October 1918. According to the historian of Knight Frank & Rutley "330,698 acres were sold for £130,000" (Jenkins, 1986, 55). The Duke in 1917 had also gifted the 12,223 acre Borgie estate to the nation to provide small holdings or crofts for ex–service-men. It was to be a rather strange sort of gift for in April 1993 it was announced that the Sutherland Estates were to have 5,000 acres of Borgie returned to their ownership. Some gift! It seems that not only the Dowager-Duchess was capable of meanness and duplicity.

In 1919 Messrs Knight Frank & Rutley were instructed to sell 114,569 acres in seven lots including that of Cambusmore with its 16,577 acres. The sale of land was to long continue and in 1977 Forsinard, where the 3rd Duke had carried out his oil extraction experiments, was also sold. Sutherland Estates, in 1874, had extended to 1,180,000 acres; by 1977 it had been reduced to 123,000 even if the Countess in a private capacity still retained another 34,500 (McEwan, nd., 25). Perhaps a perceived shortage of land had made it desirable to retrieve Borgie (or maybe there is oil in Sutherland after all!).

The 1st Duke's great marble statue in Dornoch Cathedral had long been considered a problem for he had once domi-nated the chancel and later was to command the nave. The congregation considered an internal porch would better serve present needs than a lofty figure from the past. The local press delighted to tell how the Duke, long loathed for his clear-ances, was himself moved out so that 'improvements' could take place. "Duke Evicted" ran the headlines. He was taken to Dunrobin where he was placed in the entrance hall while his plinth stands pathetic and figureless in the gardens.

For a time Dunrobin served as a residential school and there have been schemes to develop part of its parkland but little has happened. Dunrobin still stands proud and undisturbed. It remains the grandest house in the North and one of the truly great houses in Scotland. Its magnificent gardens, fascinating museum and palatial rooms have made an old castle into a popular tourist venue. Visitors flock to see its treasures but they will search in vain for any items which belonged to Duchess Blair. She has been expunged from the castle's story. Her spirit had been exorcised.

But what of Carbisdale itself?

It still stands proudly on its majestic site overlooking the Kyle. Floodlit at night it is one of the most splendid sights in the Highlands. Tours are organised to show visitors round its stately rooms and it is still the grandest youth hostel in the land.

The estate has now been given over to forestry but that does not mean it has only interest for the forester, botanist, or naturalist. Those who simply enjoy walking will not be disappointed for it is quite different from any other Highland walks and those who revel in Scottish history can relive the dramatic events of 1650.

There is a woodland walk round Carbisdale along a good path with coloured marker posts to define the route, and much of it is by the banks of a burn, but it is rather an eerie walk. Unlike most Highland burns which are lively this one is a mere trickle and sadly so disgustingly and thickly black that it looks like a stream of treacle. There is virtually no sign of animal life – no birds sing, not a single rabbit scurries away and even the trees seem to be sapped of all vitality. A deathly aura prevails. The walk, however, is not without its attraction for it does lead to a pleasant little lochan, formerly the old mill dam, which has nearby a sturdy timber footbridge known as the 'Montrose Bridge'. At another spot on the route a timber viewpoint platform – the Montrose View – has also been provided. Both the bridge and the platform were constructed in 1987 by the Officer Training Corps of Glasgow and Strathclyde Universities.

The viewpoint offers magnificent views of both the battlefield and Kyle and a seat has been provided at either side of the platform to allow the visitor to sit back and enjoy the scene. An information panel displays a plan of the battlefield and tells the visitor of the action and the significance of this historic spot. Carbisdale is without doubt a major historic spot. It may not have been a very great battle but it was a decisive one as far as the course of Scottish history was concerned. It marked the end of Montrose's military career and was the first of the stages to the scaffold.

There are two great ironies to the tale.

Tongue Lodge had been a shooting box built for Duchess Blair when she had prospects in Sutherland and it had caused much family friction when it was being built. She was to be denied it after the 3rd Duke's death and it was to remain the property of the Dukes of Sutherland. It was, in 1946, leased to the Scottish Youth Hostels Association who were to purchase it in 1958. The SYHA therefore have two properties which were built for Duchess Blair. The one in Sutherland which she was later denied and the one which she built and which only offered a prospect of Sutherland.

The Sutherland family had not wished Duchess Blair to have property in Sutherland and she had been compelled to buy land outwith Sutherland. She did the next best thing and bought land overlooking Sutherland. Reorganisation of local government in 1975 altered the old county boundaries and moved Carbisdale from Ross and Cromarty and placed it in the District of Sutherland. The Dowager-Duchess's great castle did at the end of the day not only have a prospect of Sutherland but had become part of Sutherland. It was a dream come true. Like Scott the Duchess might justly permit herself to "look back, and smile at perils past".

There seems little doubt that subsequent events would have

brought a wry smile to a certain Dowager-Duchess. She had after all secured part of Sutherland and even with the next round of reform it looks as if there are no plans to remove Carbisdale from Sutherland. It has always been part of the Sutherland story and although Duchess Blair was denied her share of Sutherland in life it is perhaps just that she should have it in perpetuity. The Duchess, it seems, has won the war.

To bring our story up to date it is necessary to make a brief return to Ben Bhraggie. The statue of the 1st Duke still offends many people and there are demands that it be toppled from the summit. Some even went to the trouble of submitting a planning application for the demolition of the monument. It should, of course, be allowed to remain. The Duke may have been a villain in his day but now he is a harmless piece of masonry. His statue is only a monument to the past but it is also the finest piece of monumental art in the Highlands.

Carbisdale Castle does not arouse animosity. It is a much-loved youth hostel, even if in need of a little more care and attention. It remains a lasting monument to an enigmatic yet rather greedy and spiteful Dowager-Duchess. It too is a monument which deserves to be cherished. It still offers a perfect prospect of Sutherland.

Bibliography

Adam, R. J. (ed).,

Sutherland Estate Management (Edinburgh: Scottish History Society, 1972)

Allibone, Jill,

George Devey-Architect 1820-1886 (Cambridge: Lutterworth Press, 1991)

Andorson, Harold F.,

Memoir of Lord Salvesen (Edinburgh: W. & R. Chambers, 1949)

Aronson, Theo.,

The King in Love: Edward VII's Mistresses (London: John Murray, 1988)

Aslet, Clive,

The Last Country Houses (London: Yale University Press, 1982)

Balfour, Lady Frances,

Ne Obliviscaris – Dinna Forget (London: Hodder & Stoughton, 1930)

Black, G. F.,

The Surnames of Scotland (New York: N.Y. Public Library, 1946)

Buchan, John,

Montrose
(Edinburgh: Thos.
Nelson & Sons, 1928)

Casson, Hugh,

Follies
(London: Chatto &
Windus, 1963)

Cushman, J. D.,

*A Goodly Heritage: The
Episcopal Church in
Florida 1821-1892*
(Gainsville: Univ. of
Florida Press, 1965)

Dixon, J. H.,

*Gairloch in N.W.
Ross-shire etc and a
Guide to Gairloch and
Loch Maree*
(Edinburgh:
Co-operative Printing
Co., 1886)

Doyle, Sir A. Conan,

*Sherlock Holmes – The
Complete Novels*
(1890-1915),
(London: Chancellor
Press, 1987)

Drummond, David,

*Taylor & Humbert
1782-1982*
(London: Taylor &
Humbert, 1982)

Forman, Sheila,

*Scottish Country Houses
& Castles*
(Glasgow: Collins,
1967)

Fraser, Sir William, *The Sutherland Book* (Edinburgh: N.P., 1892)

Gifford, John, *Highlands and Islands (The Buildings of Scotland)* (London: Penguin, 1992)

Girouard, Mark, *The Victorian Country House* (London: Yale University Press, 1979)

Groome, Francis, *Ordance Gazetteer of Scotland* (London: Wm. Mackenzie, n.d. but 1885)

Hanham, H J., *Elections and Party Management, Politics in the Time of Disraeli and Gladstone* (Brighton: Harvester Press, 1978)

Headley, G. & Meulenkemp, W., *Follies* (London: Jonathan Cape, 1986)

Heath, James, (J. H.), *A Full Relation . . . of the Great Victorie Obtained Against the Marquis of Montrose* (Edinburgh: 1650)

Hough, Richard,

Edward & Alexandra:
Their Private and Public
Lives
(London: Hodder &
Stoughton, 1992)

Jenkins, Alan,

Men of Property
Knight Frank & Rutley
(London: Quiller Press,
1986)

Jones, Barbara,

Follies and Grottoes
(London: Constable,
1974)

Langtry, Lillie,

The Days I Knew
(London: Hutchinson,
1925)

Lawson, J. P.,

Hostels for Hikers
(Stirling: SYHA, 1981)

MacEwan, John,

Who Owns Scotland?
(Edinburgh: EUSPB,
1977)

Macgregor, Alasdair Alpin,

Land of the Mountain &
the Flood
(London; Michael
Joseph, 1965)

Macgregor, Alasdair Alpin,

The Goat Wife –
Portrait of a Village
(London: Wm.
Heinemann, 1939)

Meller, Hugh,   *Castle Drogo*
                                   (London: National
                                   Trust, 1992)

Michell, Arthur Thomson,   *Five Generations of the*
                                   Family of Blair
                                   (Exeter: Wm. Pollard,
                                   1895)

Moncrieffe, Sir Iain,   *The Highland Clans*
                                   (London: Barrie &
                                   Jenkins, 1982)

Morris, W. J. (ed),   *Foliejon Park: a Short*
                                   History
                                   (Mining and Chemical
                                   Products, n.d. but 1970)

Mott, George,   *Follies and Pleasure*
                                   Pavilions
                                   (London: Pavilion,
                                   1989)

Oatts, Lt. Col. L. B.,   *Proud Heritage*
                                   (Edinburgh: Nelson,
                                   1952)

Oliver. J. L. E.,   *The History &*
                                   Development of Holloway
                                   Prison From 1849-1990
                                   (London: HM Prison
                                   Holloway, 1990)

Page, William, (ed.),   *Victoria History of the*
                                   County of York – North
                                   Riding
                                   (London: St Catherine
                                   Press, 1923).

Paget, Warburga, Lady,

Embassies of Other Days (London: Hutchinson & Co., 1928)

Pattison, Mark.

Memoirs (London: Cassell, 1988)

Pearsall, Ronald,

Conan Doyle – A Biographical Solution (Glasgow: Richard Drew Publishing, 1989)

Percy, C, & Ridley, J, (eds.),

The Letters of Edwin Lutyens (London: Collins, 1985)

Polson, Alexander,

Gairloch & Wester Ross (Dingwall: Geo. Souter, 1908)

Powell, C. G.,

An Economic History of the British Building Industry (London: Architectural Press, 1980)

Read, Donald.

Edwardian England (London: Harrap, 1972)

Reid, Stuart,

The Campaigns of Montrose (Edinburgh: Mercat Press, 1990)

Richards, Eric,   *The Leviathan of Wealth*
                                   (London: Routledge &
                                   Kegan Paul, 1973)

Robinson, John Martin,   *The Latest Country
                                   Houses*
                                   (London: Bodley Head,
                                   1983)

Ross, Susan,   *The Castles of Scotland*
                                   (Edinburgh: Chambers,
                                   1987)

Stuart, Denis,   *Dear Duchess –
                                   Millicent
                                   Duchess of Sutherland
                                   1867–1955*
                                   (London: Victor
                                   Gollancz Ltd., 1982)

Sutherland, Duke of,   *Looking Back*
                                   (London: Odhams
                                   Press, 1957)

Sutherland, Duke and Duchess of,   *Record of Events about
                                   Quarrel between
                                   Themselves and Lord
                                   Stafford*
                                   (Trentham: privately
                                   printed, 1892).
                                   Copy in Staffordshire
                                   Records Office

Vlamplew, Wray,   *Salvesen of Leith*
                                   (Edinburgh: Scottish
                                   Academic Press, 1980)

DIRECTORIES, SERIALS AND YEARBOOKS

Dictionary of National Biography
Who was Who

Burkes Peerage
Kelly's Directory
SYHA Handbook
Slater's Directory

JOURNALS AND NEWSPAPERS

The Builder
Building News
The Evening Times
The Glasgow Herald
Graphic
The Illustrated London News
The Inverness Courier
The Ladies Pictorial
The Moray & Nairn Express
The Northern Times
The Perthshire Advertiser
The RIBA Journal
The Scotsman
The Scots Magazine
The Scottish Field
Scottish Law Reporter
Scottish Youth Hostels Association Newsletter
The Times